Turning back to God

Hosea and Obadiah simply explained

Michael Bentley

EP BOOKS
1st Floor Venture House, 6 Silver Court, Watchmead,
Welwyn Garden City, UK, AL7 1TS

web: http://www.epbooks.org
e-mail: admin@epbooks.org

EP Books are distributed in the USA by:
JPL Distribution
3741 Linden Avenue Southeast
Grand Rapids, MI 49548

E-mail: orders@jplbooks.com
Tel: 877.683.6935

First published 2000
This edition 2017

Unless otherwise indicated, Scripture quotations in this publication
are from the Holy Bible, New International Version. Copyright © 1973,
1978, 1984, International Bible Society. Used by permission of Hodder &
Stoughton, a member of the Hodder Headline Group. All rights reserved.

British Library Cataloguing in Publication Data
ISBN: 978-0-85234-450-7

To JOHN APPLEBY,
pastor, missionary author and literary editor,
who persuaded me to attend a conference in 1976
where I met Jennifer,
who later became my wife.
In my biased opinion this is John's greatest achievement.

Contents

Obadiah

Foreword

The so-called 'Minor Prophets' continue to be largely overlooked in the contemporary evangelical church. In a generation which is given over to the quest for immediacy, and above all 'relevance', not a few preachers would think hard and long, but then decide against preaching a sermon, let alone a series, from the books of Hosea and Obadiah. They seem to belong to a world that is so remote from our own and, on the surface, to deal with issues so dissimilar from those which we face, that both Bible readers and Bible preachers decide to 'pass by on the other side'. We are much the poorer as a result.

So it is a special treat to welcome this exposition of the two books, and to commend Michael Bentley's careful explanation and application of the Old Testament material so persuasively for the contemporary church. Here we have both the largest of the pre-exilic Minor Prophets (Hosea) and the shortest (Obadiah) within the one volume. Hosea's demanding life and ministry were carried out against the background of a world dominated by the Assyrian Empire and its ruthless war machine. A son of the northern kingdom, he was called by

God to proclaim his mercy and judgement over many years as the mighty Assyrian ruler, Tiglath-Pileser III, extended the boundaries of his realm, bringing Israel and her usurper-king, Menahem, on to his list of vassals. Threatened from without and torn by internal divisions, Israel was a patient in terminal decline, eventually falling to the Assyrian army at Samaria in 722 BC. Into the closing years of this long process God sent his messenger to remind his people of his covenant marriage with them, of his faithful love which would not let them get away with their sin, which he must judge, and of the horrors of the covenant curses becoming their experience instead of the blessings he had longed to give them.

Obadiah's task was rather different. While the date of his little book is difficult to determine, its message comes with equally crystal clarity. Edom—symbolic of the nations ranged against the Lord and his people—will be judged by God. It seems that when the prophecy is given, Jerusalem and the southern kingdom have already fallen to the Babylonians (587–6 BC). But the disappearance of Israel and Judah from the political map should not cause God's enemies to exult. They have not accomplished such devastation; it is God's righteous wrath against his people's rebellion.

Both prophets came to teach the unchanging character of the covenant LORD to a deaf and careless people. Like all the other prophets of the Old Testament, they stand on the foundation of the law (Torah) to declare the inevitability of the faithful God's fulfilment of his covenant promises, just as he had declared he would. As mediators between God and the people, the prophets are called to preach this unchanging message, to call covenant people back to their obligations of covenant obedience, to set before them blessings and cursings, the choice between life and death. In the midst of all the uncertainties and unpredictability of the tides of human history, the rock of God's sovereign immutability stands, immovable and totally dominant. That was what covenant people needed to know then, as the remnant of faithful believers seemed, at times, to have been reduced to a totally insignificant stump. Yet out of that stump came the shoot and branch of Jesse, great David's greater Son, the Messiah, our Lord Jesus Christ, with his great fulfilment of all God's promises in the work of redemption and the creation of the new universal people of God.

It is exactly the same message which New Covenant people need to hear and heed. The weakness of the churches in our generation is largely due to our ignorance of the character of our God. And where do you go, in the Bible, to see that character more clearly expounded than in the ministry of the prophets? If the church neglects to listen to God's word of self-revelation in the prophets, we shall be condemned to a superficial sentimentalism in our view of God, which will be blown away, like dust, in the storms of life. Those readers of Michael Bentley's previous contributions to the Welwyn Commentary Series will not need further recommendation to dig with him into this rich mine of Old Testament treasure. It is to be hoped that many for whom these two books have been closed, and perhaps a little forbidding, will find a sure guide in these studies, which will lead, not only to personal benefits, but to their proclamation with authority and confidence in many a pulpit.

David Jackman
Director of the Cornhill Training Course
London

Hosea

Introduction to Hosea

Hosea is the first of the twelve books known as the Minor Prophets (they are only minor in the sense that they are much shorter than the prophecies of Isaiah, Jeremiah and Ezekiel). He was the only one of the writing prophets to come from the northern kingdom of Israel (which is sometimes called Ephraim, or Samaria, after the name of its capital city).

We know nothing about the life of Hosea apart from the information given in this book. He was the son of Beeri and he prophesied somewhere around the middle of the eighth century BC. His ministry began shortly after that of Amos. Amos has a great deal to say about God's judgement coming upon Israel, but Hosea actually identifies the enemy as Assyria (7:11; 8:9; 10:6; 11:11).

Hosea prophesied during the reigns of the kings named in the opening verse of the book that bears his name. Although his message was directed almost exclusively to the northern kingdom, the kings identified are in the main those of the southern kingdom of Judah.

Hosea lived during the turbulent days of the six kings of

Israel who followed Jeroboam ll (see 2 Kings 15:8-31; 17:1-41). During these thirty-eight years or so, the power of Assyria was growing and seeking to expand westwards. To ward off the threat of invasion, King Menahem paid tribute to the King of Assyria (2 Kings 15:19-20), but shortly afterwards, in 733 BC, Israel collapsed and only a small part of the kingdom remained free. In 722-721 the Assyrians finally captured Samaria and deported the population, thus bringing the northern kingdom to an end.

The book of Hosea divides into two parts—chapters 1-3 and 4-14. In the first of these divisions Hosea briefly describes his marriage to an adulterous woman and makes the connection with Israel's unfaithfulness to God. From chapter 4 onwards this dramatic, personal beginning is not mentioned again. However, it broods over the rest of the prophecy as Hosea paints a picture of God's deep love, his disappointment and anger, and his determination to persevere with his 'unfaithful wife'—the people of Israel.

As we study this book we shall encounter many serious issues, not least the incredible waywardness of God's people in the face of his willingness to forgive the sin of those who will return to him with genuine and humble repentance. We shall also take especial notice of Hosea's own experiences with his unfaithful wife; he still loved her and wanted her back, despite her inconstancy.

This book is filled with emotion. It has great relevance for God's people today, many of whom regularly wander away from the Lord. It has a powerful message for busy or bored Christians who feel the temptation to leave their wives or husbands and go after other (much more exciting) partners.

We cannot read this prophecy without tears in our eyes and an ache in our hearts. May the study of its truth lead us to a more fervent love for the Lord and a stronger desire to obey his Word.

1

A man made for a happy domestic life

Please read Hosea 1:1–2

When the average well-brought-up young man leaves home and starts out into life, there are few things that he desires. He has passed through the stage of wanting everything his friends have got, and he now thinks about those matters that he sees as essential to his happiness— such as a good, secure, satisfying job which is reasonably well paid; a comfortable, if not lavish, home; a loving wife and agreeable children.

Hosea probably had similar ambitions when he set out into adult life. We know nothing about his circumstances. He does not appear to have been a priest, nor, like his contemporary Amos, a shepherd. In fact, we know nothing at all about him except that he had a great and very deep love for God and for his people.

In the eleventh chapter of his prophecy it is God who is

speaking, but we sense that the prophet shares the longings of
his Lord:

> When Israel was a child, I loved him,
>   and out of Egypt I called my son ...
> I led them with cords of human kindness,
>   with ties of love;
> I lifted the yoke from their neck
>   and bent down to feed them   (Hosea 11:1,4).

We can see, then, that Hosea was someone who, to all
appearances, was 'made for a happy domestic life'. Yet this
was not to be; God had other plans for him. Right at the very
beginning of his ministry, the Lord called him to do something
which was to bring him, and his family, a great deal of
unhappiness. However, before we discuss this in more detail, we
need first to consider the times in which he prophesied.

God called Hosea to be a prophet

At the very beginning of his book we read, 'The word of the
LORD ... came to Hosea son of Beeri' (1:1). He received authority
to proclaim God's Word. Just as the word of the Lord came to
Joel (Joel 1:1), Micah (Micah 1:1) and Zechariah (Zechariah 1:1), so
it also came to Hosea. God called Hosea to pass on the message
of the Lord to all the people.

However, the message of Hosea's prophecy did not merely
apply to his own generation. The fact that his prophecy is
quoted many times in the New Testament proves that. Hosea
1:10 is quoted in Romans 9:26. Hosea 2:23 is quoted in 1 Peter
2:10 and Romans 9:25. Hosea 6:6 is quoted in Matthew 9:13
and in Matthew 12:7. Hosea 10:8 is quoted in Luke 23:30 and in
Revelation 6:16. Hosea 13:14 is quoted in 1 Corinthians 15:55.

From this list of quotations we can see that this prophecy not
only spoke to Israel 2,500 years ago; it is the eternal Word of

God, and it has great relevance for the people of God in all ages, including our own.

God called Hosea when things were bad in the land

The Lord called Hosea to warn the people of God's impending judgement upon them because of their immorality. This was going to be a very difficult task for the prophet because he loved his land dearly. Henry Cook says, 'Israel was his motherland, and always when he speaks there is a sob in his throat.'

The word 'Hosea' means 'salvation'. It is another form of the name 'Joshua'.

We are told in Hosea 1:1 of the various kings in whose reigns the prophet did his work. If we add up the total length of time these men reigned, then it would seem that Hosea prophesied over a period of some thirty-eight years. (The precise length of the reigns of the kings of Judah and Israel can often be confusing because some of their reigns overlapped.)

By the time God called on Hosea to speak up, the land had been divided into two: Israel lay to the north and Judah to the south of the country. Many years before the time of our prophet, after the death of Solomon, God divided the land as a punishment for the sinfulness of the people. Although God's people still lived in both parts of the land, there was a deep division among them, and this was never to be healed.

Hosea belonged to the northern kingdom. Of the other writing prophets, only Amos lived in that part of the country, and even he came from the southern kingdom. The north was also the area where Elijah and Elisha had done their work some eighty years before the time of Hosea. However, the utterances of these earlier prophets were never collected into a book.

The southern kingdom was called Judah and just two and

a half tribes inhabited it. The other nine and a half tribes (commonly called 'the ten tribes') were in the north. The northern kingdom went under various names. It was usually called 'Israel', but, as we noted in the introduction, sometimes it was referred to as 'Ephraim' (after the most powerful of the tribes living there) and on other occasions it was called 'Samaria' (after the name of its capital city).

However, the fact that God's people were divided into two nations was not the greatest problem that Hosea had to cope with. It was the character of the kings who reigned during his period of office, and their influence on the people, which caused him so much distress.

In Hosea 1:1, four kings of Judah are named, but only one from Israel: 'The word of the LORD that came to Hosea son of Beeri during the reigns of Uzziah, Jotham, Ahaz and Hezekiah, kings of Judah, and during the reign of Jeroboam son of Joash king of Israel.' Most of these kings were unhelpful, and some were positively wicked. Although Uzziah was a friend of the southern kingdom prophet Isaiah, he was not wholly a good king. He came to the throne when he was sixteen years old and reigned for fifty-two years (2 Chronicles 26:3). He started well, and did many things that were right in the eyes of the Lord, but his popularity and his success caused him to be too proud. Therefore, as a punishment, he was struck with a terrible leprosy which plagued him for the rest of his life (2 Chronicles 26:21).

The second king mentioned, Jotham, did what was right in the eyes of the Lord, just like his father, Uzziah. However, his zeal petered out when it came to doing something about the heathen altars in the land. Just like so many people today, he did not have the courage to tackle the things that were really a stumbling-block to the people. Although he did do some useful rebuilding work on the temple, he did not try to confront the real issues that were afflicting his kingdom.

Ahaz, the third king, was an out-and-out unbelieving man. It is recorded of him that 'He did not do what was right in the eyes of the LORD' (2 Kings 16:2-3). This is how he behaved: in order to appease the heathen gods he gave his own son as a human sacrifice (2 Kings 16:2-3), and he turned away from the worship of the Lord and started to engage in the immoral worship of northern Israel (2 Kings 16:4).

The fourth Judean king mentioned, Hezekiah, was a very much better king: he *did* love God. Unlike his predecessors, he set to work to rid the land of everything that had been used in pagan worship. It is written of him, 'Hezekiah trusted in the LORD, the God of Israel ... He held fast to the LORD and did not cease to follow him ...' (2 Kings 18:5-6).

The fifth king mentioned reigned in the northern kingdom of Israel. He was Jeroboam, the son of Josiah (sometimes called Jeroboam II). He was also on the throne for a long time, which is why only one king of Israel is mentioned during the period of Hosea's prophecy. The land prospered during his reign but, sadly, he continued in the evil footsteps of the first Jeroboam: 'He did evil in the eyes of the LORD and did not turn away from any of the sins of Jeroboam son of Nebat, which he had caused Israel to commit' (2 Kings 14:24).

Heathen idol-worship was rife in Israel. The land was filled with shrines to the fertility gods, or Baals, and asherahs, dedicated to female deities, were found in many places. However, the condition of the land was not the greatest evil that Hosea had to endure.

God called Hosea to do an exceedingly difficult thing

Hosea received a most puzzling message from God. He was a

fine, upright, moral man, and the words of Hosea 1:2 must have come to him, as they do to us, like a bombshell. The Lord said to Hosea, 'Go, take to yourself an adulterous wife and children of unfaithfulness, because the land is guilty of the vilest adultery in departing from the LORD.'

Getting married is not something which anyone should undertake lightly, or thoughtlessly. The marriage service tells us this, and so does common sense. There are so many marriage breakdowns in these days that everyone should be doubly careful to whom they link themselves in marriage, which is, or ought to be, for life. However, here we see God telling Hosea the woman he was to marry. The amazing thing is that she was the most unlikely kind of person for a religious man, or any believer, to wed. God describes her as 'an adulterous wife'.

We cannot be certain whether Gomer already had children when Hosea married her, or whether the words, 'children of unfaithfulness', refer to children who were yet to be born. However, we can imagine how Hosea must have felt when he received this message. Quite clearly, from the way he writes, he had a heart filled with love, but on the very first occasion that the Lord began to speak to him, he told him to marry a woman whom God himself describes as an adulterous woman. Therefore, if Hosea obeyed God and married her, he could be certain that he would have a very trying time ahead of him, because it was not sensible to start off married life with someone who had such an immoral history.

Maybe Hosea thought that if he obeyed God then everything would go well with him and his marriage would run smoothly. On the other hand, he may have remembered Joseph, who did what was right, yet ended up in prison for maintaining his integrity and moral purity. If we had been in Hosea's position, what would we have done? We should probably have thought that we had misheard what the Lord was calling us to do, because we know that he requires us to live a godly, moral life, obeying his commandments, including the one which says, 'Do not commit adultery.'

God often told his prophets to do strange things. Elijah had to pour four large jars of water over his sacrifice on Mount Carmel before lighting the fire under it (1 Kings 18:30–35). Ahijah tore his new cloak into twelve pieces and gave ten of them to Jeroboam (1 Kings 11:29–32). Ezekiel had to do numerous things which seem peculiar to us (e.g. Ezekiel 4:1–6). Strange though this instruction from God must have seemed to him, Hosea obeyed and married Gomer, the daughter of Diblaim, despite the anxiety, and maybe even the taunts, of his friends. (We are given these little biographical details, of her name and parentage, to show us that these were real people, who actually lived.) Notwithstanding the doubts he must have had about the matter, Hosea did as God commanded him, and in so doing he opened up his life to many years of misery.

God used Hosea to demonstrate his displeasure with his people

Why did God go to such lengths to get his message over to the people? Why did he not simply use preaching to bring the land to its senses? Calvin concludes that it was because the 'diseases of the people were incurable ... [and] the state of things was almost past recovery'. Therefore God chose Hosea to undergo this indignity so that the people could see how their God was suffering because of the spiritual adultery of his people.

They had been saved from the bondage of Egypt. They had been led, as a nation, through the desert and brought to the promised land. But instead of showing love, and persevering in commitment, to their God who had done so much for them, they had turned their backs on the one true God and had prostituted themselves to other, false, gods.

There are many ways in which God's people today have been guilty of spiritual adultery. We have to confess that we are no better than Israel of old. When we consider the situation of Hosea, we are forced to realize how sinful we are in turning for our pleasure to other 'gods', those of our own day and age, and turning our backs on the Lord God who loves us and cares for us.

2

The effects of spiritual adultery

Please read Hosea 1:2–2:1

Someone once said that 'A Christian should so live that he would not be afraid to sell the family parrot to the town gossip.' Home life is so very important. How we live at home will have a great influence on our children. Therefore parents should always try to act wisely because children watch every move they make, and will copy what they see them do.

The prophet Hosea had a number of children, and as his wife was promiscuous we cannot be sure, any more than he was, that he was the father of all of them. However, he faced up to his responsibilities to bring up his children in the ways of the Lord, to the best of his ability.

We are told about three of the children in Hosea's home. The first one was born to him (1:3), but we are not told who was the father of the other two. What we *are* informed of is that God himself gave a name to each of these children. The reason why he gave them these particular names was so that the whole nation (both the northern kingdom of Israel and the southern kingdom of Judah) could take warning from them—and so that they might be induced to amend their adulterous ways.

God warned that he would punish the people

When the first child was born God said, 'Call him Jezreel' (1:4). Jezreel was the name of a well-known town and also a valley in the northern kingdom. Its 'location ... in a valley-plain between the mountains of Samaria and Galilee, and its close proximity to the valley of Megiddo, mark it as one of the prominent battle sites in Palestine, one of the few places where chariotry, cavalry and marching armies could be manoeuvred'.

Many famous battles had been fought at Jezreel. It was here that Gideon had defeated the Midianites. The Bible records the incident: 'Now all the Midianites, Amalekites and other eastern peoples joined forces and crossed over the Jordan and camped in the Valley of Jezreel' (Judges 6:33). The story tells us how, with only three hundred men, and in the power of the Lord, Gideon won a great victory. The people of Israel would also have known that it was in this vicinity that the slaughter of the house of Ahab had been carried out by God's orders (2 Kings 9).

The mention of Jezreel would have brought back to the minds of the people the wickedness of King Ahab and his wife Jezebel. Ahab had met his just deserts. He had been a thoroughly bad king, who had not only allowed Jezebel to establish Baal worship throughout the land (1 Kings 16:31), but had also connived at the execution of Naboth, merely because he wanted Naboth's vineyard for his own pleasure and use (1 Kings 21).

Therefore, every time the people of Israel looked at young Jezreel they would have been reminded that he was named after a place of terrible bloodshed. It was at Jezreel that King Jehu had inflicted a terrible massacre on the household of Ahab and the former kings of Israel. It is true that he killed these people at God's command; in fact, the Lord commended him for his obedience. This was because God wanted all these people to be destroyed because they were steeped in Baal worship. He ordered that these heathen practices be eradicated from the land. So Jehu undertook this carnage, and he was rewarded by God's promise that his descendants would reign in the land until the fourth generation (2 Kings 10:30).

The question arises, then: 'If God commended Jehu, why did he tell Hosea that he would "punish the house of Jehu for [this] massacre"?' (Hosea 1:4). It was because Jehu had revelled in this bloodshed. It is certainly true that wrongdoers should be punished, but no one ought to take delight in inflicting punishment. God himself says, 'As surely as I live ... I take no pleasure in the death of the wicked.' The Lord does not take pleasure in revenge. He desires that evil people should turn from their ways and live (Ezekiel 33:11). It is essential that we should warn people that they are in danger of going to the everlasting punishment of hell unless they repent and turn to God. However, we should never speak of such judgement without tears in our eyes.

Jehu did not act like that. He took great pleasure in killing hundreds of people. Furthermore, he only carried out half of what God told him to do. He certainly destroyed the shrines of Baal, but we read in 2 Kings, 'However, he did not turn away from the sins of Jeroboam son of Nebat, which he had caused Israel to commit—the worship of the golden calves at Bethel and Daniel' In addition we are told, 'Yet Jehu was not careful to keep the law of the LORD, the God of Israel, with all his heart. He did not turn away from the sins of Jeroboam, which he had caused Israel to commit' (2 Kings 10:29,31).

God also told Hosea some very bad news about the northern

kingdom. He said, 'I will put an end to the kingdom of Israel' (1:4). This little boy, Jezreel, was to be the sign that God would do this. Then, to make doubly sure that Hosea understood, he added, 'In that day I will break Israel's bow in the Valley of Jezreel' (1:5). In Psalm 46 we read, 'He [God] makes wars cease to the ends of the earth; he breaks the bow and shatters the spear, he burns the shields with fire' (Psalm 46:9). The bow was one of the foremost weapons of war in those days. On this occasion it was not the bow of the heathen invader which was going to be broken; it was the bow—that is, the might—of Israel. God's people were going to be defeated in that same Valley of Jezreel where so many had met their end in the past. This was going to take place when the Assyrian army invaded the land with evil intent.

Israel would not be able to rely on the fact that they were God's people, nor would they be able to trust in their own military might (their bows etc.). The next time God was *not* going to save them. Everything came to pass just as God said it would. In 733 BC, 'An Assyrian army fought its way into this valley and lopped off the northern territories of Israel, marching their inhabitants off to Assyria' (see 2 Kings 15:29).

Thus it was that Israel's bow was broken in the Valley of Jezreel, and this happened because 'The land [was] guilty of the vilest adultery in departing from the LORD' (1:2). Therefore, those who were proud to be called the people of God ought to have been spoken to by the name given to this little boy, Jezreel. The name Jezreel means 'God scatters'. It even sounds something like the name 'Israel'. And so it proved to be: Israel became Jezreel; God's people became those whom God scattered. This was solely because they refused to repent of their spiritual adultery.

However, before that happened two more children were born

into Hosea's family. Like Jezreel, these children were also given in order that the people would have further opportunities to repent of their sins.

God's threat to withdraw his love and his name
We then learn that 'Gomer conceived again and gave birth to a daughter' (1:6). We are not told whether this second child was born to Hosea, as we were in the case of Jezreel (1:3). She may have been his, or someone else may have been the father.

The Lord again gave Hosea very unusual instructions concerning this second child. He said, 'Call her Lo-Ruhamah.' This means 'Not loved'. This was an awful name to give to a little girl. Yet God gave instructions that she must be called this because, he said, 'I will no longer show love to the house of Israel, that I should at all forgive them' (1:6).

We see, then, that not only was God going to break Israel's bow in the Valley of Jezreel and put an end to the kingdom of Israel, he was also going to stop loving them. This was very serious because God had told Moses on the mountain about his love for his people. He had passed in front of Moses and proclaimed, 'The LORD, the LORD, the compassionate and gracious God'. He had also said that he was 'slow to anger, abounding in love and faithfulness, maintaining love to thousands, and forgiving wickedness, rebellion and sin' (Exodus 34:6–7).

What had happened to God's promise? Had he forgotten the covenant that he had made with the house of Israel? (See, e.g., Exodus 34:10). No, he had not forgotten. In fact, over the years he had forgiven their wickedness, rebellion and sin time without number. But Israel had failed to keep their side of the agreement. They had not fulfilled the conditions of the covenant that he made with them on the mount. Instead they had been unfaithful to him and had departed from him by turning to other gods. Or, as Jeremiah was to put it:

> My people have committed two sins:
> They have forsaken me,
>   the spring of living water,
> and have dug their own cisterns,
>   broken cisterns that cannot hold water   (Jeremiah 2:13).

But the Lord was gracious to his wayward people; he was slow to inflict punishment upon them. He had given them Jezreel as a sign, which ought to have brought them to their senses. However, still they did not take warning from the boy's birth—or rather from his name! So now God gave them a further alert, and this was another child, one given the name 'Not loved'.

Despite this second warning, they still refused to take notice, or to do anything about their backsliding. God therefore adds something further. Although he says that he will 'no longer show love to the house of Israel', that is, to the northern kingdom, he also tells them, by way of contrast, 'Yet I will show love to the house of Judah [i.e. the southern kingdom]; and I will save them—not by bow, sword or battle, or by horses and horsemen, but by the LORD their God' (1:7).

God was going to withhold his punishment from the southern kingdom for a further hundred years. This was not because they were more godly than those in the north were; it was solely because he chose to do so. He wanted to encourage Israel to repent, so that they too would be saved from the dreaded Assyrian invaders. Judah was going to be protected, not by their own efforts, but by the Lord their God. Much later in their history, when the Jews returned from exile in Babylon, the Lord told them that he would help them in their difficult task of rebuilding the temple, and that they would carry out the work 'not by might nor by power, but by my Spirit' (Zechariah 4:6).

But none of these things brought the Israelites back to the Lord. So we read, 'After she had weaned Lo-Ruhamah, Gomer had another son. Then the LORD said, "Call him Lo-Ammi, for you are not my people, and I am not your God"'(1:8–9). These words would have sounded dreadful to any who were spiritually sensitive among the people. God had told them, 'You are not my people, but those of Judah are my people.' Something even worse was to follow: 'And I am *not* your God.'

Can Hosea have understood correctly? Had God not spoken kindly to Moses and the Israelites? Had he not said, 'I am the LORD, and I will bring you out from under the yoke of the Egyptians. I will free you from being slaves to them, and I will redeem you with an outstretched arm and with mighty acts of judgement. I will take you as my own people, and I will be your God'? (Exodus 6:6–7).

No, Hosea had not misheard what God was saying. The people had gone so deeply into sin that they were going to be cast off. One day, quite soon, the Assyrian army would swoop down in judgement upon them and carry them off as captives. From this captivity they would never return. The Lord gave them each of these signs because he wanted the people to be so distressed when they realized this that they would come to their senses and turn away from their idols—and cast themselves on God's mercy.

Is it not amazing how stubborn they were in failing to respond to God's urging for them to return to him? It almost beggars belief that they could carry on in their own sweet way, and ignore the Lord's call to turn aside. Yet are we, today, any better? Are we aware that God is serious when he speaks about the danger of being outside his kingdom? Do we know what it is to be far off from God, and not to be really enjoying all the pleasures of this life, and yet fail to respond to his call to repent and come to him?

God offers hope to his disobedient people

It is now Hosea's voice that we hear (rather than God speaking directly—although the prophet is relaying the voice of God). What he says sounds at first like a contradiction of what has gone before, but it is not. It is the voice of love which speaks. It is the voice of God's grace, echoed in Hosea's speech: 'Yet the Israelites will be like the sand on the seashore, which cannot be measured or counted. In the place where it was said to them, "You are not my people", they will be called "sons of the living God"' (1:10).

He goes on: 'The people of Judah and the people of Israel will be reunited, and they will appoint one leader and will come up out of the land, for great will be the day of Jezreel' (1:11). Then he adds, 'Say of your brothers, "My people", and of your sisters, "My loved one"' (2:1).

Do you recognize that phrase about the Israelites being like sand on the seashore? That was the same promise as was made to Abraham after he had sacrificed the ram in place of his son on Mount Moriah, and that was subsequently repeated to Jacob (Genesis 22:17; cf. 32:12). So, despite the sin of God's people, the pledge that had been made to them so many times in the past would be fulfilled.

Certainly the people of Israel were going to be taken away to Assyria, but the nation was going to survive. Isaiah tells us how that would come about. He says that a remnant would endure and they would multiply and become a great nation:

In that day [the day of God's grace and power] the remnant of
Israel,
    the survivors of the house of Jacob,
will no longer rely on him
    who struck them down [the Assyrians]
but will truly rely on the LORD,
    the Holy One of Israel   (Isaiah 10:20).

How will they grow into such a great nation that they cannot
be numbered? It will be by God's grace, and also by the gathering
in of the Gentiles. Paul explains to us in Romans 9:25–26:

As [God] says in Hosea,

'I will call them "my people" who are not my people;
    and I will call her "my loved one" who is not my loved one,'

and [says Paul],

'It will happen that in the very place where it was said to
them,
    "You are not my people,"
they will be called "sons of the living God".'

We see, then, that God, by one stroke of his gracious pen, has
struck out the word 'not' from the record. The people of Judah
and the people of Israel, who had been divided for so long, will
be reunited. They will appoint one leader who will come up out
of the land.

Later in Hosea he goes on to tell us who that great leader
will be. In 3:5 we read, 'Afterwards the Israelites will return and
seek the LORD their God and David their king.' But David was
no longer alive. In his famous address on the Day of Pentecost
Peter said, 'Brothers, I can tell you confidently that the patriarch
David died and was buried, and his tomb is here to this day' (Acts
2:29). True, but this David will be great David's greater Son. It is

the Lord Jesus Christ who is able to bring about this miracle of
grace. When he hung on the cross of Calvary his blood washed
out that awful word 'not'. Although no one deserves it, when
believers come to put their trust in Christ they are transformed
from being those who are *not* the people of God and *not* loved by
God. Instead he now says of them, 'You *are* "my people" and "my
loved one".' The word *'Lo'* has been taken from *Lo-Ruhamah* and
Lo-Ammi. God's blood-bought people are now *Ruhamah* ('loved')
and *Ammi* ('my people').

He then speaks about the day of Jezreel being 'great'. Jezreel
means 'God scatters', but it also carries the sense of 'God sows'.
In those days the farmer sowed his seeds by scattering them. So
God scatters his people, then he sows them and cares for them
so that they can grow up to become a precious plant for his glory
(see Isaiah 11:1).

When we come to look at Hosea 2:22–23 we shall read:

... the earth will respond to the grain,
   the new wine and oil,
   and they will respond to Jezreel.
I will plant her for myself in the land;
   I will show my love to the one I called 'Not my loved one'.
   I will say to those called 'Not my people', 'You are my people';
   and they will say, 'You are my God.'

That is what God does for his own redeemed people in every
age. Those who have long been sunk deeply in sin, and all their
lives have been unaware of God's grace, will, through Christ's
redeeming blood, be 'born again' and washed from every stain
of their iniquity. In the same way, those who have backslidden
from the ways of God will return to his paths. This will not be
because they have performed some religious deed, or indulged
in any particular good work; it will be solely by God's grace and

love. All believers will be so overwhelmed with the blessings of God that they will be overflowing with adoration and praise to the God who acts so wonderfully on behalf of such unworthy children.

3

The wages of unfaithfulness

Please read Hosea 2:2–13

Have you ever noticed how many miserable people there are in the world? You can find them in the supermarket queue. You hear them on the radio and television, and you can meet them in the street. Some mornings you leave home feeling quite cheerful, and yet when you stop and talk to a person like this a dark cloud comes over you, and you return home feeling depressed.

But of all the miserable people around there are none so sad as backsliders, as those who once came to know the Lord as their Saviour and Friend, but have now gone back on their profession of faith in Christ. They are cast down because they have once known the joy of salvation, but have now drifted far away from God.

Bishop Ryle, writing in the last century, said, 'It is a miserable thing to be a backslider. Of all unhappy things that can befall a man, I suppose it is the worst. A stranded ship, an eagle with a broken wing, a garden covered with weeds, a harp without strings, a church in ruins—all these are sad sights, but a backslider is a sadder sight still.'

The book of Hosea is about backsliding. We have already seen that the prophet Hosea was directed by God to marry an adulterous woman, so that the people of Israel might come to see the consequences of their unfaithfulness to God. He told them, 'The land is guilty of the vilest adultery in departing from the LORD' (1:2).

Now, in this chapter, we shall see some of the ways in which Israel had gone away from the Lord, and what he was going to do as a consequence of their unfaithfulness to the covenant that he had made with them.

This section of Hosea's prophecy can be seen at three levels. It is all about the faithful one and the adulterer. At the first level Hosea is the faithful husband and Gomer is the adulterous wife. At the second level God is the one who is faithful to his promise, and Israel is the nation who has turned away from her God and prostituted herself with other gods. And at the third level our God is the one who is always faithful to his word, and we are those who have forgotten him and have been disobedient to his commands.

God pleads with his children, Israel (2:2–3)
In the guise of a human husband's wretchedness as he gathers his children around him to speak about the unfaithfulness of their mother, God addresses his people. Whenever one of their parents forsakes the other, the children cannot help being affected. Everything that we do in a family affects everyone in that household. When a marriage breaks down the children usually suffer a great deal. In the verses before us we find God talking to his people. He speaks some difficult words to them:

'Rebuke your mother, rebuke her.' Then he gives the reason: 'For she is not my wife, and I am not her husband.'

Do these words mean that Hosea had divorced Gomer? No, he had not done so. We know this because, under the Mosaic law, if he had divorced her then he would never have been able to take her back again (see Deuteronomy 24:4). But Hosea 3 tells us that the two of them came back together again. What he was saying, then, was this: 'Your behaviour has shattered the intimacy which we once enjoyed. We are no longer living as husband and wife together.' Although no divorce had taken place, the relationship had failed. Just as Hosea's purpose in speaking to his children like this was to see if Gomer would take more notice of them than they did of him, so God pleads with his children. Hosea desperately wanted his wife back; the Lord also longs for his people to return to him. But certain conditions had to be fulfilled before Hosea would take Gomer back again.

Some people have experienced the agony of having their marriage partners back after they have left them, only to find that they leave again after a short while. Because of this kind of situation Hosea realized that it was very important to lay down the conditions for Gomer's return. This is why he said, 'Let her remove the adulterous look from her face and the unfaithfulness from between her breasts' (2:2). Before she came home she had to do two things. In the first place, she had to get rid of the paint and powder plastered all over her face, because these had emphasized her availability to anyone who would pay sufficient money for her favours. Secondly, she was to take away 'the unfaithfulness from between her breasts'. Those breasts, which had once given suck to Hosea's children, were, in her unfaithfulness, decorated with gaudy jewellery (see 2:13). It was essential, then, that Gomer should be made modest once again before Hosea could welcome her back into his home.

However, that was not all. The children were to speak even more severely to their mother. They were to inform her what Hosea would do if she failed to comply with his wishes. The prophet was so desperate to have his wife back that he even gave his children this message: 'Otherwise [unless she does this] I will strip her naked and make her as bare as on the day she was born' (2:3). Gomer, as a harlot, was prepared to appear naked before her lovers, because they rewarded her for her daring; but for her to be publicly exposed was an act of extreme humiliation—even for a prostitute!

What a terrible thing it must have been for Hosea to instruct the children to tell their mother this! Why, then, did he inflict such pain upon his children? It was because he was so desperate that he was prepared to resort to any lengths to have Gomer back again in a proper relationship as his wife. It was not so much that he enjoyed the thought of inflicting shame upon Gomer. It was that he loved her so much that he would go to *any lengths* to get her back—even at the risk of harming his relationship with his children!

Many have gone through the agony of being prepared to do *anything* in order to save their marriages, yet have received nothing but rejection for their efforts!

God appeals to Israel (2:3–8)
The Israelites had backslidden. They had behaved just like an unfaithful wife in a marriage. They had turned their backs upon the one who had saved them and provided for all their needs. Instead of showing gratitude they had lusted after other gods— the Baals. They did this because they thought these heathen gods would grant them much material gain.

The Baals were fertility gods, and the people certainly needed their crops to grow and produce a plentiful harvest. This is why they bowed down to the altars of Baal with the hope of getting a plentiful harvest. It is not surprising that God, their Redeemer, was displeased about their behaviour. That is why he said of Israel, 'I will ... make her as bare as on the day she was born.'

But when was this nation of Israel born? It was when the Lord brought the people out of Egypt with a mighty outstretched hand (Psalm 77:15; see also Ezekiel 16:4–8). At that time they were in the desert, which was a parched land, and they were dying with thirst. Ezekiel 16:4–7 gives a very vivid picture of Israel at the time of her birth as a nation, in which she is described as a new-born infant left unwashed and 'kicking about in your blood'. In speaking through Hosea in this way, God wanted to remind the Israelites of all that he had done for them since he had rescued them from the slavery of Egypt and brought them into this promised land. He warns them that he will inflict the same conditions on them again, unless they return to him.

In verses 4 and 5 God describes how Israel had committed spiritual adultery and had given birth to children out of wedlock. She had turned her back upon the Lord (as Gomer had deserted Hosea) and had gone after other lovers. Why had she done that? What does a prostitute get out of her work? It is not excitement, and certainly not pleasure. I suspect there is very little job satisfaction either. A prostitute engages in her business solely to gain material possessions.

The problem is that these material things only last for a little while. Israel had the same experience. She went after her lovers (the heathen gods) to get food, water, wool, linen and drink. Israel was interested in what she could get *for herself.* That is why Hosea says, '[Their mother] said, "I will go after my lovers, who give me my food and my water, my wool and my linen, my oil and my drink"' (She continually says 'my', 'my', 'my'). Israel actually believed that it was her lovers (the heathen gods) who could provide for her needs. This is the reason why she said these material things are 'mine'.

However, God was angry with this behaviour. In verse 8 he reminded Israel of some solemn facts. He said, 'She has not acknowledged that I was the one who gave her the grain, the new wine and oil, who lavished on her the silver and gold.' What did the people use these things for? They made the silver and the gold into idols. That is why God complains, 'I gave them these things, which they used for Baal.'

God warns Israel (2:9–13)

It is God's turn to do something now. All along it has been Israel who has been setting the pace, but from now onwards we see God announcing that he will act in six different ways.

1. He will block up the way

In verse 6 and again in verse 9 he says, 'Therefore' (cf. also 2:14; 13:3). He makes it clear that he is not going to stand idly by while his people do as they please. First of all, he says, 'I will block her path with thorn-bushes; I will wall her in so that she cannot find her way.' The consequence of his action will be that 'She will chase after her lovers but not catch them; she will look for them but not find them.'

Israel thought that she could do just whatever she liked, but God told her that he was going to block up the way. He would do it with prickly bushes. On hearing this she appears to come to her senses. 'All right', she says, 'I will go back to my husband as at first, for then I was better off than now' (2:7). She seems to recognize the folly of her actions. Her lovers had turned away from her when they were tired of her, or her beauty began to fade. So now she says, 'I was better off with my husband.'

This kind of talk reminds us of the prodigal son when he

came to his senses. He said, 'How many of my father's hired men have food to spare, and here I am starving to death! I will set out and go back to my father and say to him: Father, I have sinned against heaven and against you. I am no longer worthy to be called your son; make me like one of your hired men' (Luke 15:17–19).

In the same way, when everything was going against Israel she said that she wanted to return to her husband—that is, to her God. We could be horrified and think to ourselves, 'She would say that, wouldn't she?' But we need to ask ourselves if we are any better than Israel. When we wander astray from God, and the Holy Spirit convicts us of our sins, the first thing that comes into our minds is: 'I would be better off if I went back to God.' But that is the language of the prostitute. That is what someone says whose desire is only for material things.

Israel said, 'I will go back,' but was God prepared to accept her? No. He was not. He was not prepared to have her back unless she showed that she had really repented of her sins. We know this because the Lord goes on to say:

> She has not acknowledged that I was the one
>   who gave her the grain, the new wine and oil,
> who lavished on her the silver and gold—
>   which they used for Baal
>
> (2:8).

Her knowledge of God was faulty.

It is here that Hosea uses the word 'know' (NIV, 'acknowledge') for the first time. This is an expression which will be used repeatedly throughout this book (see 2:20; 4:1,6; 5:4; 6:3,6; 13:4). 'To know' is a verb which is used to refer to the greatest intimacy in marriage (the same word is used of Adam's relationship to Eve before the birth of their sons, see

Genesis 4:1,25, AV). '[This word] ... captures the essence of his understanding of what God wants and what Israel is lacking. Intimacy, loyalty and obedience—the threefold cord of the covenant—are braided together in this word.'

2. He will take away his gifts
The second thing that God is going to do to bring Israel back to her senses is to take something away. He tells her, 'I will take away my grain when it ripens' (2:9). The people thought that worship of the Baals would ensure a good supply of grain, but God reminds them that it is he who provides this. It is his grain.

3. He will expose her for all to see
The third thing that God is going to do in punishment is to 'expose her lewdness' (2:10). He will 'take back [his] wool and [his] linen', which had been 'intended to cover her nakedness'. This means that because of her unfaithfulness to him and his Word, he was going to leave her exposed. She would be laid bare to all the elements. And she would be left uncovered so that all who passed by would see her as she really was. When her nakedness was revealed to her lovers, they would reject her.

Hosea tells Israel that 'No one will take her out of [God's] hands' (2:10). None of the Baals will be able to take them from the clutches of God's punishment. Nor will they want to. In fact, they are only lifeless idols. Even a backslider still belongs to God.

4. He will put a stop to the festivals
The fourth thing that God will do to Israel is to 'stop all her celebrations' (2:11). Joy and gladness were all part of Israel's festivals. Throughout the first five books of the Bible the Israelites were enjoined to keep the various feasts to his glory. For example, in Exodus 23:14-17 we read, 'Three times a year you are to celebrate a festival to me. Celebrate the Feast of Unleavened Bread; for seven days eat bread made without

yeast, as I commanded you. Do this at the appointed time in the
month of Abib, for in that month you came out of Egypt. No
one is to appear before me empty-handed. Celebrate the Feast
of Harvest with the first-fruits of the crops you sow in your
field. Celebrate the Feast of Ingathering at the end of the year,
when you gather in your crops from the field. Three times a year
all the men are to appear before the Sovereign LORD.' Also the
Sabbath days were especially to be observed.

These things were not chores for the Israelites. They did not
just do them out of habit. They were a definite benefit to them.
But now God says, 'I will stop all her celebrations: her yearly
festivals, her New Moons, her Sabbath days—all her appointed
feasts' (2:11).

5. He will ruin the crops

The fifth thing that God will do to Israel is 'ruin her vines and
her fig trees' (2:12). This produce was what the people needed to
trade with. Instead of these fruits, 'which she said were her pay
from her lovers', doing them any good, God was going to take
the crops and do something to them. He said, 'I will make them
a thicket.' He had said a similar thing in verse 6. In that earlier
verse he was going to block Israel's way with thorn-bushes. The
people had wrongly attributed the provision of crops to the
Baals, and as a result they would see wild animals devour the
fruit of their labours.

6. He will punish the nation for her infidelity

Finally, God is going to punish Israel 'for the days she burned
incense to the Baals' (2:13). She had been very occupied in
decking herself out in 'rings and jewellery'. She enjoyed dressing
up and she went after her lovers. But what does God say about
her actions? The most devastating statement comes right at the
end of verse 13, where we read, '"But me she forgot," declares the
LORD.' Israel was in a very bad way. She had reached the point

where she had lost her knowledge of the Lord. And, like any backslider, she had lost the joy of the Lord.

God speaks to us today

Why have we spent all this time looking at what God said to this nation some 2,700 years ago? We have seen how badly they behaved. We have rightly been horrified. We have observed that, although God had provided so much for these people, they had turned away from him and turned instead towards other gods.

But are we any better? Jeremiah wanted to know why the people had turned away in perpetual apostasy (Jeremiah 8:5). God wants to know why *we* have turned aside from him and his love.

Those who have once tasted that the Lord is gracious have experienced a time when they have confessed their sins to God and discovered his forgiveness. At that time they were very elated because they knew that God had saved them and made them into real Christians. They told everyone how they had been saved. They went eagerly down into the waters of baptism. In those early days they were bright, glowing witnesses to God's grace in their lives. But now things are rather different. Like the psalmist, they want to cry out, 'Restore to me the joy of your salvation' (Psalm 51:12), or to echo William Cowper's sigh:

> Where is the blessedness I knew
> When first I saw the Lord?
> Where is the soul-refreshing view
> Of Jesus and his word?

The central message of this passage is that we need to return to the Lord. Gloom and the threat of punishment are not all there is in Hosea chapter 2. In our next chapter we shall go on to see that there is a door of hope (2:15), and that hope is available for those who confess their waywardness to the Lord and return to him. It was when the Lord Jesus Christ died on the cruel cross that he opened up the way to deal with sin.

4

A fresh start

Please read Hosea 2:14–23

In our studies so far we have seen that Hosea not only passed through a time when his wife largely ignored him, but he found out what it was like to discover that she had gone after other lovers; she had behaved as a prostitute. God used the breakdown of the relationship between Hosea and his wife Gomer to show Israel the true situation between himself and his people. He told them that they, too, were behaving like a harlot. This was because they had turned their backs upon him and had turned aside to worship other gods—the Baals, or fertility gods, of the land of Canaan.

In 2:2–13 we saw that God had outlined some of the things that he would do by way of punishment in order to bring the Israelites to their senses. He sought to persuade them to come back into a right relationship with himself. He said:

> I will punish her [Israel] for the days
>   she burned incense to the Baals;

she decked herself with rings and jewellery,
    and went after her lovers,
    but me she forgot   (2:13).

In this chapter we are going on to see how God reacts in view of their appalling behaviour.

A new hope (2:14–17)

Before we examine the passage let us think about how we would react if our wife, or husband, had behaved as Israel had done towards their God. We would be very angry indeed, and we would threaten all kinds of punishments. Even though we still loved our partner, we would feel humiliated. We would certainly be anxious about going out of the house in case we met any of our friends or acquaintances. Our fear would be that they would laugh at us for not being able to keep our spouse under control. The consequence of this would be that we would want to creep away and hide our face in shame because our marriage partner had brought great disgrace upon our home and family. Everyone would think of us as being incredibly weak and unable to control or influence our husband or wife.

However, God, the Lord Almighty, who reigns in justice, does not act like that when he is faced with the unfaithfulness of his people. Instead he says, 'Therefore [in view of her behaviour] I am now going to allure her; I will lead her into the desert and speak tenderly to her' (2:14). Surprisingly, he treats Israel with great kindness. He says he is going to woo her again—to win back her love.

Why, then, does he say that he will lead her into the desert? Deserts are very hot and barren places. Little vegetation grows there. They are places of harshness and bitterness. The reason why the Lord says this is because it was in the desert that God found Israel in the beginning of her nationhood.

A later prophet, Jeremiah, was going to say something similar to the people of Jerusalem:

I remember the devotion of your youth,
　　how as a bride you loved me
and followed me through the desert,
　　through a land not sown   (Jeremiah 2:2).

Therefore, in order to bring the Israelites back to himself, God tells them he is going to take them back to the desert.

He reminds them of the time when he rescued them from the cruel slavery of Egypt. Just as human lovers like to go back to the place where they first met, so God tells his people that he is going to lead them through that same desert where he rescued them.

In a spiritual sense it does us all good to go back, in our thoughts, to the place where we first met the Lord. Those were the days described by the Lord himself as the time of 'first love' (cf. Revelation 2:4). Even though the outward situation might have been very bleak for us as we bowed down under the burden of our sin, for the very first time in our lives we came face to face with our Saviour and Friend. That is the joy of salvation, and it is to that experience that we, as believers in the Lord Jesus Christ, should continually look back, especially when we are in a fearful state, or in danger of going astray from the paths of the Lord.

Jesus said, 'I, when I am lifted up from the earth, will draw all men to myself' (John 12:32). God says, in a similar vein, 'I am … going to allure her' (Hosea 2:14). His people are going to have great joy, such as they expressed in 'the song of deliverance' in Exodus 15.

But the Lord is not only going to take Israel, in their memories, back to the place where they first came into a right

relationship with him. He is going to restore to them some of
the blessings which they had lost through their going astray
after other gods. He tells them:

> There [in the desert] I will give her back her vineyards,
>   and will make the Valley of Achor a door of hope.
> There she will sing as in the days of her youth,
>   as in the day she came up out of Egypt   (2:15).

In 2:12 he had told them that he was going to ruin their vines.
Now he says that one day (when they come back into a right
relationship with him) he will give these vineyards back to them.
That is what happens when people return to the Lord. In Joel
2:25 God tells his people, 'I will restore to you the years that the
... locust has eaten' (NKJV).

When the Israelites eventually emerged from their long years
of wandering in the desert they suffered their first defeat at
a little village called Ai, which was near Jericho. It happened
because of the greed of a man called Achan, who kept for himself
some of the spoils of war. He was caught and punished by being
stoned to death (with his entire household). When he was dead,
he was buried under a huge pile of stones at a place called the
Valley of Achor. This was situated near the north-west end of
the Dead Sea (Joshua 7:1–27). The valley was given that name,
which means 'the Valley of Trouble', as a result of these events.
It was a place of defeat and, as such, it remained as a permanent
reminder to everyone of what the Lord will do to those who
misuse his blessings.

However, through Hosea, God now tells the people that one
day he will restore his grace to them. At that time the Valley
(or door) of Achor (trouble) will become 'a door of hope'. In
other words, it was through trouble that blessing would come
to them. That is often what happens in a material, and also in

a spiritual, sense to those who come back to the Lord. When a person is saved he or she often has first to pass through a deep valley of sorrow. Some people have to go through a time of very deep conviction of their sin before they can enter into the joy of salvation. It is then that they cry out to God, 'I'm far too sinful for you to have mercy on me!' But the wonderful thing is that God is gracious to them. And so, particularly for such people, the door of trouble does become a door of hope. We have an example of this on the Day of Pentecost. Before those 3,000 people were saved, 'They were cut to the heart and said ..., "Brothers, what shall we do?"' (Acts 2:37).

In verse 16 the Lord tells the Israelites how their lives are going to be changed one day. '"In that day," declares the LORD, "you will call me 'my husband'; you will no longer call me 'my master'."' God had been a husband to his people (just as Hosea had been the husband of Gomer). One day that broken relationship is going to be restored. Not only that, but Israel is no longer going to call God 'my master', or (to use the Hebrew) 'my Baal'; he goes even further and says, 'I will remove the names of the Baals from her lips; no longer will their names be invoked' (2:17). There is going to be a time when Israel will come to her senses; she is going to return to the Lord. Of necessity that will mean that she will turn her back upon these Baals of the land.

A new covenant (2:18)
Hosea then proceeded to explain some more of the implications of the Day of the Lord:

> In that day I will make a covenant for them
> > with the beasts of the field and the birds of the air
> > and the creatures that move along the ground.
> Bow and sword and battle
> > I will abolish from the land,
> > so that all may lie down in safety   (2:18).

The people of Israel had broken the old covenant, which God had made with them at Sinai; they had failed to keep the Ten Commandments. However, God now promised a new covenant. Jeremiah outlines this more fully:

'The time is coming,' declares the LORD,
    'when I will make a new covenant
with the house of Israel
    and with the house of Judah.
It will not be like the covenant
    I made with their forefathers
when I took them by the hand
    to lead them out of Egypt,
because they broke my covenant,
    though I was a husband to them,'
                         declares the LORD.
'This is the covenant that I will make with the house of Israel
    after that time,' declares the LORD.
'I will put my law in their minds
    and write it on their hearts.
I will be their God,
    and they will be my people.
No longer will a man teach his neighbour,
    or a man his brother, saying, "Know the LORD,"
because they will all know me,
    from the least of them to the greatest,'
                         declares the LORD.
'For I will forgive their wickedness
    and will remember their sins no more' (Jeremiah 31:31–34).

Some of those blessings were brought in when Jesus died on the cross of Calvary. We know that because all who truly repent of their sins and turn to Christ for salvation do experience the forgiveness of sins. But at the moment we cannot honestly say that all wars have ceased. Nor have all animals agreed to live peaceably with all creation—certainly not tigers in captivity! Such fierce beasts still behave like the wild animals mentioned in Hosea 2:12. But there is a wonderful day coming when true and lasting peace will be brought in. It will be the Day of the Lord. Isaiah tells us about that day:

> The wolf will live with the lamb,
> > the leopard will lie down with the goat,
> the calf and the lion and the yearling together;
> > and a little child will lead them.
> The cow will feed with the bear,
> > their young will lie down together,
> > and the lion will eat straw like the ox.
> The infant will play near the hole of the cobra,
> > and the young child put his hand into the viper's nest.
> They will neither harm nor destroy
> > on all my holy mountain,
> for the earth will be full of the knowledge of the LORD
> > as the waters cover the sea　　　　(Isaiah 11:6–9).

On that day God will destroy this present evil world and bring in a new heaven and a new earth, which will be the home of righteousness (see 2 Peter 3:13).

However, that is not all there is to say about the blessings God will bring in.

A new courtship (2:19–20)

This same God who will allure his people and draw them back to himself will also betroth them to him for ever. He tells them:

> I will betroth you to me for ever;
> > I will betroth you in righteousness and justice,
> > in love and compassion.

> I will betroth you in faithfulness,
>   and you will acknowledge the LORD　　　　(2:19–20).

In 2:8 we read that Israel did not acknowledge the Lord, but there is a day coming when she will know the Lord. Just as Adam knew his wife, Eve, so God's people are going to know the Lord permanently and intimately. He tells Israel that he will bless her with a fivefold gift.

1. Righteousness

The first blessing is righteousness; this is a gift of God. We have all broken God's laws; we are sinners. Therefore we are not righteous. But in Jesus, and through his sacrifice on the cross, he has taken away our sins and has clothed us in his own righteousness.

2. Justice

Secondly, the Lord will bless his people with justice. God's justice takes all the unfairness away from our salvation. It is not fair that God should choose us and save us, but he does, in Christ. Because Christ has taken our guilt upon him, then our salvation becomes just in God's sight and we are justified (made right with God).

3. Love

Thirdly, God betroths his people to him in love. This is 'the love and loyalty which partners in marriage or in covenant owe to one another'. God's love for undeserving sinners is something that is so incredible that no one can fathom its depths. We can only fall in wonder at his feet and cry, 'Why have you granted such wonderful love to someone as worthless as me?'

4. Compassion

Fourthly, he promises to bless his people with compassion. Lo-Ruhamah was not pitied, but now she is going to be pitied. God will have great compassion upon her. On that day the Lord is going to reverse the awful name he gave to this child, and she will experience his great loving mercy.

5. Faithfulness

Fifthly, God is going to betroth Israel to him in faithfulness. Despite the fact that Israel had been unfaithful to God, their gracious God was still going to be faithful to them. It was Gomer's unfaithfulness that put most strain on Hosea's marriage. Yet, as we shall see in chapter 3, Hosea eventually bought her back again. In just the same way God is going to redeem Israel back. He is going to do that in his faithfulness.

A new relationship (2:21-23)

We read what God will do about the situation:

'In that day I will respond,'
   declares the LORD—
'I will respond to the skies,
   and they will respond to the earth;
and the earth will respond to the grain,
   the new wine and oil,
   and they will respond to Jezreel.
I will plant her for myself in the land'   (2:21-23).

Achor and Jezreel were two valleys which spoke of Israel's failure. 'All that is going to be changed.' 'I will show my love to the one I called "Not my loved one". I will say to those called "Not my people", "You are my people"; and they will say, "You are my God."'

Therefore, as a result of God's blessing upon Israel he is going to give them *a resplendent harvest* of corn (see comments about Jezreel on Hosea 1:4). Just as the earth will respond by producing a good crop when we get the agricultural conditions right, so God will grant his people a spiritual harvest when their spiritual situation is sound. This will not be a literal harvest of grain, wine or oil, but one of precious souls who will come to the foot of the cross, confess their sin and seek God's salvation.

Not only that, there is also going to be *a restored relationship*. God is going to show his love to those who had been cast off. He said:

> I will plant her [Israel] for myself in the land.
> I will show my love to the one I called 'Not my loved one'.
> I will say to those called 'Not my people', 'You are my people';
> and they will say, 'You are my God'   (2:23).

Throughout the prophets we read of Israel's restoration. But we also see that the Gentiles will be included in this as well. Jesus taught that 'Many will come from the east and the west, and will take their places at the feast with Abraham, Isaac and Jacob in the kingdom of heaven' (Matthew 8:11). In saying this he 'appears to redefine and extend the very meaning of the "restoration of Israel" in terms of the Gentiles'. Paul does the same thing in Romans 9:24–26 (see comments on Hosea 1:10).

However, there is a personal side to this promise as well. When believers wander off from God he says that he will come after them. He is going to draw them back into his loving arms. We all have our valleys of Achor—times when our sin brings us into great trouble. But this is the good news: there is a door of hope. Jesus said, 'I am the door. If anyone enters by me, he will be saved … I have come that they may have life, and that they may have it more abundantly' (John 10: 9–10, NKJV).

Those who come to Christ become a new creation: 'The old has gone, the new has come! All this is from God, who reconciled us to himself through Christ' (2 Corinthians 5:17–18).

5

God's love for second-hand people

Please read Hosea 3:1–5

Try to put yourselves in Hosea's shoes and ask yourself, 'How would I feel if my wife had not only turned her back upon me and my love for her, but had been unfaithful to me as well?' Gomer had taken other lovers, many of them. And we can imagine how thoroughly miserable Hosea must have been about the whole sorry business; it would have affected him badly. He would have tried everything that he could think of to bring his wife to her senses. He desperately wanted her back in a right relationship with him. But whatever he did, she persisted in her waywardness.

This is the kind of thing that happens so often in our day. Perhaps not very many wives or husbands become prostitutes, but huge numbers of them are promiscuous, and this often leads to a complete breakdown of the marriage, with separation and divorce as the inevitable result.

As we read Hosea 3:2, we get the impression that Gomer had

sunk so low in the mire that she had gone past the stage of being excited about her lifestyle; it appears that matters were now going very badly with her. Perhaps her good looks had begun to fade. Maybe a lifestyle of late nights and loose morals had started to have an adverse effect on her body, and awful diseases had started to eat away at her because of the way she had been living and loving. Possibly she was now looking extremely haggard and was at the end of her tether.

If you were in Hosea's position and had heard the news that your wife was languishing in some dark, indecent brothel, what would you think? Most people's reaction would almost certainly be: 'I hate her for the way she's behaved. She's got what she deserved.' They would want to ask her how she could do such a thing. If this had happened to you, you would very probably want to move house to another town and get as far away from her as possible. You would want to start a new life and try to forget everything about her. Many people whose marriages have broken down can sympathize with Hosea and feel deeply for him.

Did Hosea forget about Gomer, as she had forsaken him? He may well have wanted to depart and have nothing more to do with her, but God had other plans for the couple. Hosea himself tells us what happened.

The love of a husband (3:1)

He tells us, 'The LORD said to me, "Go, show your love to your wife again."' Some translations render this, 'Go again, love [her].' This is so different from the words of God's original call for Hosea to marry this woman. In 1:2 the Lord said to him, 'Go, take [her].' That is almost the kind of language that would be used of a client's relationship with a prostitute. But now, despite the way that Gomer had treated her husband, God tells Hosea to 'love' her, to 'love [her] *again*'. This is an incredible thing for

God to call upon Hosea to do. Hosea is to love his wife again, even though she is loved by another, and, worse still, '[she] is an adulteress'. The word 'again' is emphasized. However badly she had behaved towards Hosea, he was to love her, and to love her *again*. He was not to let her atrocious conduct affect the way he would love her in the future.

There is even more: Hosea is told to love his wayward wife 'as the LORD loves the Israelites, though they turn to other gods and love the sacred raisin cakes' (3:2). It is at this point that we see something of the love which lies in God's heart. Israel had treated the Lord abominably. In spite of all he had done for his people, they ignored him. They not only refused to honour him; they had turned to other gods and worshipped the Baals. The reason they did this was because they thought they could get something for themselves. That is so often why people backslide away from God. They want to get something out of their religion. Their own selfishness comes to the fore. They give the impression that they do not really go to church to worship God. They only go so that they can 'be blessed' and have an enjoyable time. The sad thing is that it is usually Christians who behave like this.

When our family first came to the church where we are now in membership, one of our unconverted neighbours started to come to our services. She said that she had tried another church, which was very much livelier than ours. However, her comment about that other church was: 'If I had wanted to go to a disco, I would have gone to one.' Although this lady did not know the Lord as her Saviour, she had no wish to go to church just for what she could get out of it!

The people of Hosea's day made no secret of the fact that they worshipped Baal for selfish reasons. They loved the 'sacred raisin cakes'. These were offerings which were made to the gods. In

Jeremiah 7:18 and 44:19 we read that God's people offered cakes of bread to a Babylonian deity called 'the Queen of Heaven'. It seems, therefore, that the Israelites found the sacred raisin cakes which were offered to the Baals more palatable than the spiritual food which the Lord God Almighty gave to them. Derek Kidner puts it in a rather amusing way: 'The bride, it seems, is only here, or anywhere else, for the cakes and ale.'

So, how does God react to all these many signs of Israel's unfaithfulness? We are told in very simple words: 'The LORD loves the Israelites.' Despite all their bad behaviour, God loved them and cared for them. He not only loved them, he wanted them back.

But how could Hosea ever forgive his wife and have her back again, after all the shame she had brought upon him—especially when he was a prophet of God? When any marriage breaks down it is a tragedy. But when the wife of a preacher of the gospel leaves her husband for another man, then it is even more humiliating. People are bound to think, 'Why did he treat her so badly that she couldn't stand him and his work any longer?' They are certain to say, 'A good husband would make sure that his wife remained on the "straight and narrow".' However, despite all of this, God said to Hosea, 'Go, show your love to your wife again.'

How could he find the grace to do such a thing? He could only do it because the Lord had commanded him to do it. Throughout the whole of their history the people of Israel had been in and out of fellowship with their Lord. Since the day they left Egypt they had either been rejoicing in the Lord's salvation, or turning aside to other gods. But each time they had been punished for their sins, they had pleaded with the Lord to forgive them. When they had repented, and promised not to go astray again, he *had* forgiven them.

How many times should any of us forgive those who treat us like that? Does there come a time when we have to say, 'Enough is enough'? Matthew records these well-known words: 'Peter came to Jesus and asked, "Lord, how many times shall I forgive my brother when he sins against me? Up to seven times?" Jesus answered, "I tell you, not seven times, but seventy-seven times"' (Matthew 18:21-22). The Lord meant that we should keep on and on forgiving anyone who is truly sorry for the way he or she has treated us.

In the same way, God forgave the wickedness of Israel. He showed his love to them once again. There is such a great emphasis on the fact that God loved his people again and again that we can only stand back and marvel at the greatness of his everlasting grace towards ungrateful, undeserving sinners.

The cost of reconciliation (3:2-3)

In these two verses we see Hosea's obedience to God. Despite his feelings of shame, he did what God told him to do and, quite simply, he records, 'So I bought her for fifteen shekels of silver and about a homer and a lethek of barley.'

Why does he tell us that he 'bought' her? Had she become someone's slave? We do not know, but possibly she had fallen on such hard times that she had been forced to sell herself into slavery. What we can be certain of is that the money that Hosea paid was the price of a slave. Exodus 21:32 stipulates that thirty shekels of silver had to be paid to the owner of a slave as compensation if someone was responsible for the accidental death of one of his slaves. From this it is generally concluded that thirty shekels of silver was the price of a slave. Here Hosea pays half of the amount in silver, and the other half in goods.

God had instructed Hosea to go and love his wife, but here we see him doing more than just telling her he loved her: we see love in action. He says, 'I bought her.' Jesus has done the same for us if we are true believers. Before we became Christians we were slaves to sin. In Romans 5:6 Paul tells us we were helpless sinners. The apostle writes to the Romans that, although we were enemies of God, we were reconciled to him through the death of his Son (Romans 5:10). God purchased our salvation with the precious blood which Christ shed on Calvary's cross. He took the initiative and stepped down and saved us. Peter puts it like this: 'For you know that it was not with perishable things such as silver or gold that you were redeemed from the empty way of life handed down to you from your forefathers, but with the precious blood of Christ, a lamb without blemish or defect' (1 Peter 1:18-19). As Calvin says, 'In some ineffable way, God loved us and yet was angry towards us at the same time, until he became reconciled to us in Christ.'

The fact that Hosea purchased Gomer did not mean that she could then do what she liked; he only took her back on certain stringent conditions. He said, 'You are to live with me for many days; you must not be a prostitute or be intimate with any man, and I will live with you' (3:3). Even though Hosea was kind to Gomer, it did not mean that he was soft towards her. He made certain stipulations with regard to her return.

She was to 'live with' him. In other words, she must not live in a loose way as she had done previously. She had to turn her back upon her old way of life. Just as formerly she had left Hosea, so now she was to leave behind her immoral lifestyle.

Secondly, she 'must not be ... intimate with any man'. This may even mean that she was to be deprived of sexual relations with Hosea himself. She had to be taught a lesson, and she had to prove to him that she had truly left behind her promiscuous ways. She had to be faithful to Hosea.

When we become Christians we are required to turn our backs upon our old, sinful way of life. We are to live a new life—one that is in strict obedience to God and his Word, the Bible. This may sound hard, but it is not. John tells us, 'This is love for God: to obey his commands.' Then he adds, in case we think that is asking too much, 'And his commands are not burdensome' (1 John 5:3). If we love God, and we receive his love into our hearts, then, like Christ himself, we shall delight to do God's will (Matthew 26:39; see also Psalm 40:6–8).

This period was to be a time of chastening for Gomer, just as Israel would have to pass through a time of severe testing twenty-five years or so after the time of this prophecy. The effects of this are amplified in the following verse.

The trials of God's people (3:4)

Hosea went on to compare the testing of his wife with the tribulations that Israel would shortly have to undergo, when the Assyrians came to take them away out of their land. He proclaimed, 'For the Israelites will live for many days without king or prince, without sacrifice or sacred stones, without ephod or idol.' Just as Gomer was to be deprived of intercourse, so Israel would exist without king or prince. They were going to be captured and deported by the cruel Assyrians. There they would have no rulers of their own.

Not only that—the worship of God, represented by the temple sacrifices, was going to be taken away from them, and certainly they would have no access to their 'sacred stones' (or pillars). These stones had been used innocently at the first (see Genesis 28:18), but by this time they had become part of Israel's depraved worship.

'For many days', in other words, for a long period of time, they were going to be 'without ephod or idol'. The ephod was a kind of waistcoat worn by the priest as part of the tabernacle worship instituted by God in the desert (Exodus 39:2–7). However, by the time of Hosea its use had been corrupted. So many things had been used idolatrously that God was going to take them all away from the people.

This punishment was all part of God's work in bringing the Israelites back to himself. Assyria was God's way of leading them into the desert (see 2:14) but, mercifully, Hosea does not dwell on this severe time of testing from which the northern kingdom would never recover.

The future of God's people (3:5)

Graciously, Hosea emphasizes the 'afterwards'. Eternal punishment is not going to be the destiny of God's people. But, so sadly, it will be the destiny of those who reach the end of their days without repenting of their sins and casting themselves upon God's mercy.

For God's people the final chapter of the story is incredibly wonderful: 'Afterwards the Israelites will return and seek the LORD their God and David their king. They will come trembling to the LORD and to his blessings in the last days.' They are going to 'return' and they are going to 'seek'. These are the blessed words that lead to eternal joy and peace. Those who leave the paths of sin and return will find that God is waiting to receive them, just as the father of the prodigal was waiting to receive his wayward son home once again (Luke 15:20). Those who seek the Lord will find him. Jeremiah tells us, 'You will seek me and find me when you seek me with all your heart' (Jeremiah 29:13).

But these wanderers are not only going to find their God; they are going to find their king as well. What does this mean? David had been dead for many years. Yet Hosea says that one day they will have their great King David reigning over them once again.

He is referring to great David's greater Son, King Jesus, the one who will 'reign for ever and ever' (Revelation 11:15).

How, then, are God's repentant people going to behave as they contemplate these future blessings? They are going to 'come trembling to the LORD'. This time when they approach him 'trembling' it will not be because they are terrified. No, they have nothing to be frightened about, because Christ has taken away their sins and they are now dressed in the robe of Christ's righteousness (Revelation 19:8). On that day they will be trembling with excitement because they are about to receive his great blessings. Even though they are undeserving, God took the initiative and sent his Son to die to pay the price of their sins. They are reconciled to God (2 Corinthians 5:19). This is what they will glory in. They will be with the Lord for ever and enjoy his peace and blessings. For them there will be 'no more death or mourning or crying or pain, for the old order of things [will have] passed away' (Revelation 21:4).

How well do you know God?

Please read Hosea 4:1–11

When we talk to people we meet about the Lord Jesus Christ, they sometimes say that they do not have time for church. Others tell us that the church is full of hypocrites. They continue, 'What I want to see is the church doing some good in the world. Why don't they sell some of those gold-plated ornaments and give the money to the poor, as Jesus told them to? What good do those churchgoers think they are they doing by sitting in their old Victorian buildings, singing out-of-date hymns to dreary tunes for hours on end?'

Of course, people who talk, or think, like that are missing the point. True religion is much more than taking part in solemn services, or debating philosophical issues; it is a matter of the heart. It has very little to do with outward ceremonial. This was where the people of Hosea's day were way off course.

Hosea lived some seven hundred years before Jesus was born. His home was in the northern part of the land, the area called

Israel. It was there that ten of the tribes of the Israelites had settled after Joshua brought them in from the desert. But now, many years later, things had gone badly wrong and the people had left behind them the true worship of their Creator and Saviour.

Amos, a great prophet of God, was preaching around the same time, and not so many years earlier the prophets Elijah and Elisha had thundered out God's call to return to him and his ways. With all this preaching, the people ought to have been brought back to a right relationship with God, but they were so fixed in their ungodly ways that they had drifted further and further away from God and the paths of righteousness.

Hosea was raised up by the Lord for this situation because he knew what it was like to be rejected by his wife in favour of others. This prophecy is a picture of Israel's unfaithful behaviour as a nation. Although they were God's own people, his special possession, they turned aside from the love of God and turned instead to worship other gods, which were no gods at all. As we come to Hosea 4 we reach the second main section of his prophecy. From now until the end of the book, we read various calls given by God, through Hosea, which ought to have brought the people back to a right relationship with him.

The state of the nation (4:1-3)

With the opening verse we are taken, in our imagination, to a court of law, but this is no ordinary place of justice; it is God's court. The defendants are the people of Israel, and they are on trial, charged with grievous crimes. Not only is this God's court, but the judge is none other than God himself. Through Hosea's preaching he has called the people to hear the accusations he has against them.

These charges are not against the wicked world as a whole;

they are directed to those 'who live in the land'. This land was very special to Israel. It is the same land that the Jews are reluctant to share with the Palestinians today. They do not even want to hand over 13% of the Jewish settlements on the West Bank. They maintain that this is land that has been given to them by God himself. The religious Jews believe that they are still God's own chosen people.

This land of Israel is the place that was often described in the Bible as the 'land flowing with milk and honey'. It was the place to which their forefathers headed as they wandered in the wilderness for some forty years in the days of Moses. That is the setting of this chapter.

In Hosea 4:1 we see that the court is in session. As we read these opening verses we see that God is prosecuting the Israelites because they have not kept his laws and the covenant which he made with them when they were in the desert.

The charge he brings against them is no light matter which can be dismissed after only a short hearing. Nor, if the people are found guilty, does it only carry with it a small fine, or a slight warning about the future. This accusation is the most serious charge that God can bring against his people, and they ought to be feeling thoroughly ashamed of themselves.

The first three points which God brings against them are to do with the failure of the people:

Hear the word of the LORD, you Israelites,
    because the LORD has a charge to bring
    against you who live in the land:
'There is no faithfulness, no love,
    no acknowledgement of God in the land'   (4:1).

No faithfulness

First of all, the people had not been faithful to God. This is very surprising because he had done so much for them. He had saved them and brought them into the very place that he had promised to them. Yet they had failed to be faithful to him, even though he had always kept his promises to them.

The Israelites were required to be faithful, to be loyal to their covenant-keeping God. Before they entered this promised land, Joshua had challenged their forefathers: 'Now fear the LORD and serve him with all faithfulness.' He had gone on to say, 'Throw away the gods your forefathers worshipped beyond the River and in Egypt, and serve the LORD' (Joshua 24:14).

The people were not only required to be faithful to their God; they were also obliged to behave honestly towards their fellow men and women. Among many other places, God summed this up in Proverbs 3:3, where he said:

Let love and faithfulness never leave you;
> bind them around your neck,
> write them on the tablet of your heart.
Then you will win favour and a good name
> in the sight of God and man.

But these things the people failed to do.

No love

Secondly, the people had failed to show love to God and their neighbours. Earlier, in Hosea 2:19, God had said that he would betroth Israel to himself 'in righteousness and justice' and also 'in love and compassion'. His people were not only recipients of his love, they were also required to love him in return. However, once again strong, steadfast love was missing from the lives of the people. The love which they should have displayed to God and to one another was given instead to the heathen gods of the land—the Baals.

No knowledge of God

Thirdly, as a consequence of these other two failures, the people failed to demonstrate that they had a knowledge of God. We see their failure to acknowledge God outlined in Hosea 5:4. When we come to examine 6:6 we shall see how God pleads for them to acknowledge him. We also saw when we looked at 2:20 that there is a time coming in the future when Israel will acknowledge the Lord.

What does it mean, 'to know God'? In Jeremiah 22:15-16 the Lord refers to Josiah and says:

> He did what was right and just,
>   so all went well with him.
> He defended the cause of the poor and needy,
>   and so all went well.

Is that not what it means to know me?

King Josiah knew the Lord, but what does knowing the Lord mean for us?

When a husband, who has been married to his wife for many years, is accused of doing something bad, the wife will often reply, 'I know my husband—and he wouldn't do that.' She knows her husband because she has been in love with him for very many years and he with her. They have been together through thick and thin, and they have no secrets from each other. We need to ask ourselves, 'Do I know God like that?' Knowing God is not just knowing *about* him. It is not merely being sure that he is alive—the demons believe that, and shudder (James 2:19). Knowing God means having a constant, intimate, personal relationship with him, just as a truly loving husband has with his wife—only it is far, far greater than that.

The state of the nation

The second three points flow out from Israel's failures. Because they had forsaken God's ways, the nation was in a terrible state. That is the sole reason for the trouble they were in. The indictment continues:

> There is only cursing, lying and murder,
>   stealing and adultery;
> they break all bounds,
>   and bloodshed follows bloodshed   (4:2).

These are some of the very things the Ten Commandments legislate against. These evils are transgressions of the ninth, sixth, eighth and seventh commandments (Exodus 20:1-17).

Two centuries before Hosea's time Jeroboam I had introduced idolatry into Israel (1 Kings 12:28-29), and now the consequences were being demonstrated for everyone to see. 'Rejection of the God of the Bible will affect society.' In these days sins which formerly used to be kept under the carpet are now openly on show. This is always the case for those who turn their backs upon the clear commands of God. Only a return from wickedness and an acknowledgement of God and his Word will rescue a person, or a nation, from the kind of judgement which eventually befell the people of Israel. And even lands which call themselves Christian are in danger of the same kind of judgement from God, because they have turned aside from his Word and his ways.

Because the people of Israel were so disobedient to God's clear commands, the land mourned (4:3). It is a dangerous thing for people to break free of all constraints. God's laws are not severe restrictions designed to spoil our fun. John tells us that they are not burdensome (1 John 5:3). The person who has an intimate, daily relationship with God finds it a delight to obey God's will. He is like the psalmist when he says, 'I desire to do your will, O my God; your law is within my heart' (Psalm 40:8).

We should all beware of false prophets who promise us freedom from all constraint. Peter tells us that such people 'are slaves of depravity' (2 Peter 2:19). Teenagers so often want to break free of parental constraint, but parents know the dangers that there are lurking in the darkness of this world. The awful consequences for the people of Hosea's time who broke their bonds were bloodshed following bloodshed (4:2). In other words, murder upon murder was the norm. But it was even worse than that: God tells us that every living thing started to die. Death is always the result of sin (Ezekiel 18:4). It was not only humans who were dying. Animals and fish were starting to waste away as well.

Where did the greatest blame lie? (4:4–6)

Whose fault was it that the land was in such a dreadful state? In situations like this people tend to reproach everyone except themselves, but Hosea makes it plain who should take the greatest blame. He aims his criticism squarely in the laps of the priests. Like Amos, he seems to have a particular priest in mind (see Amos 7). This charge against the high priest is enlarged to include all the priests. In fact, both the priests and the prophets have fallen. Hosea tells us that they 'stumble day and night'. These people ought to have been living in ways that were holy and were helpful to others, but they fell short of the standards which they should have been setting for everyone to follow. They were just like the religious people of the days of Jesus. They were blind leaders of the blind (Matthew 15:14).

The appalling consequences of their failure were that people were destroyed. This note of destruction comes again and

again in this passage. The land mourns. Those who live in it are
wasting away and even the animal population is dying (4:3). This
note of devastation continues. The Lord tells these unworthy
priests, 'I will destroy your mother' (4:5). By their 'mother' he
means Israel as a nation. Therefore, because of the sinful ways of
the people, even those of God's own people, the nation of Israel
was going to be crushed. That actually happened at the time
when the Assyrians took them away captive, never to return.
This is why the northern kingdom is so often referred to as 'the
ten lost tribes'.

Why were the people going to be destroyed? It was because
they lacked knowledge. It could be argued, 'But these were the
people of God. Surely if anyone knew the Word of the Lord,
they would have done.' However, the sad fact was that there
was 'no acknowledgement of God in the land' (4:1). And the
reason for this was that the priests were not teaching the people
the ways of righteousness. They had rejected the Word of God
themselves, and so they saw no reason to teach it to the people.
That was why the northern kingdom was going to be destroyed.
It was because of their lack of knowledge.

We, too, in our day, are in great danger of being punished
for our lack of knowledge of the Word of God. Lloyd Ogilvie
writes, 'We are not destroyed by a lack of education, but rather
by a lack of in-depth study of the Scriptures, prayer, and living
out the truth of God's revealed will in our lives. Consequently,
our character is shaped by cultural values and not knowledge of
God.'

God's sentence against the priests (4:6–11)
God is very severe in his denunciation of the religious leaders.
Those who hold any office in the church of God are required to
act responsibly in their duties. It is no light thing to serve God.
Those who have positions of authority must take great care

that they serve God to the very best of their ability. They must not lord it over those who are entrusted to them, but must be 'examples to the flock' (1 Peter 5:3). The Word of God does not countenance any form of 'heavy shepherding'.

Because the priests 'ignored', or forgot, 'the law of [their] God', God was going to 'ignore', or forget, their 'children'. Their progeny would be diminished. In both the natural and the spiritual sense, their children were going to be reduced in number. The more priests there were, the more they sinned against God.

'They exchanged their Glory for something disgraceful.' In other words, the blessing which they should have received in carrying out God's will was going to be turned to shame by the Lord. This was because they were more interested in exalting themselves than in honouring God and feeding the people with the Word of God.

Ezekiel denounces those who should have been shepherds of Israel. He says, 'The word of the LORD came to me: "Son of man, prophesy against the shepherds of Israel; prophesy and say to them: 'This is what the Sovereign LORD says: Woe to the shepherds of Israel who only take care of themselves! Should not shepherds take care of the flock?'"' (Ezekiel 34:1-2).

Instead of leading the people away from wickedness, these priests relished their wickedness (4:8). This was because the more the people sinned, the more choice lambs they brought for sacrifice, and every time a sacrifice was made the priests were allowed to keep a portion of the meat (see Leviticus 6:25-26; 10:17; cf. 1 Samuel 2:13-17). The priests thought that they were on to a good thing. But God said, 'They will eat but not have enough; they will engage in prostitution but not increase.' The reason for all this lack of progress was 'because they have deserted the LORD' and given themselves instead 'to prostitution, to old wine and new'. These things all 'take away the understanding of [the] people'. As Hosea puts it in 4:9, it is a case of 'like people, like priests'. The people only get the priests they deserve.

The warning for us today
What can we learn from this solemn passage? It teaches us that God is Judge, and he will punish all those who are unrepentant. These people showed no remorse at all for their wickedness. They had no desire to return to God. Therefore they were going to be destroyed. The same thing will happen to all those who die in their sins. It is a sad indictment on God's people today that those who are in places of authority are in many cases not leading the people into the ways of God. So many of the laws of Britain that used to reflect the teaching of the Bible have now been overturned. The religious leaders of our nation are more interested in trying to build a society based on pleasing everyone than on obeying the clear teaching of the Word of God.

Each of us needs to confess that we have fallen far short of God's standards. There is no acknowledgement of God in our land. We have prostituted ourselves by turning aside to bow down to the gods of this world and worship them, rather than obeying the one true and living God. And we have gorged ourselves with the 'good things' of this life which have deadened our understanding of the ways and will of our God.

The only hope for our nation, and for us as individuals, is for us to fall on our knees and confess our sin to our Almighty God and Father. We need to plead for him to have mercy upon us. How wonderful that the Word of God declares, 'If we confess our sins, [God] is faithful and just and will forgive us our sins and purify us from all unrighteousness' (1 John 1:9). And 'If we walk in the light, as he is in the light, we have fellowship with one another, and the blood of Jesus, his Son, purifies us from all sin' (1 John 1:7).

7

How stubborn are you?

Please read Hosea 4:12–19

One of the things I loved to do when I was a child was to go to the cattle market which was regularly held near my home. Some of us children found it fun to go and see the sheep and cows being unloaded from the train to be transported to the nearby market. The cattle trucks would be shunted into the siding and lorries would be backed up to the doors. A ramp would then be set up, linking the cattle truck to the rear of the lorries, and someone with a stick would go into each truck in turn and drive the sheep out. They usually went placidly enough, following the animal in front of them. But sometimes it was a different story, especially with the cows—particularly the young heifers. Things would go quite smoothly until, every now and then, one of the young animals would try to make a bolt for it. Their eyes would glaze over with fear and, as they saw a possible way of escape, they went for it. Sometimes one managed to run all over the goods yard and it would take quite a few men to capture it. We youngsters thought that was fun, but the men responsible for the animals had a different view of the matter!

I thought of this childhood memory as I read this passage where Hosea described the Israelites as 'stubborn, like a stubborn heifer'. The prophet meant that they were like those cows I remember from my youth. They were difficult to handle and they refused to comply with God's laws.

Moses had found their forefathers prone to the same thing when they were wandering through the desert. God told him, 'Your people, whom you brought up out of Egypt, have become corrupt. They have been quick to turn away from what I commanded them and have made themselves an idol cast in the shape of a calf. They have bowed down to it and sacrificed to it and have said, "These are your gods, O Israel, who brought you up out of Egypt."' The Lord went on: 'I have seen these people ... and they are a stiff-necked people' (Exodus 32:7-9).

Almost a thousand years later, in the days of Hosea, we find that they were still behaving in similar ways. God's people were continuing to be rebellious; they remained stubbornly obstinate in their determination to go their own way.

They refused to seek the Lord (4:12)

In verses 4-11 of this chapter God's main attack is against the priests. In his law court he is accusing the people of going astray. They had refused to acknowledge the Lord and the reason for this was that they had not taken the trouble to get to know the Lord, or to study and obey his Word.

These priests not only failed to carry out their duties; they also spent their time indulging in all kinds of immoral and ungodly activities. Although they ate of the best meat of the sacrifices which the people brought, they were always hungry for more. Although they indulged their sexual lusts to the full—and did so in the name of religion—their families did not increase in number. And although they enjoyed large quantities of both old and new wine (which fermented very quickly), they were no wiser. Instead they lost what little understanding they had in the first place. This all happened because they had deserted the Lord (4:10–11).

Obviously their behaviour had a severe effect on the people. These priests were meant to be the religious leaders of the community. They should have set a good moral and spiritual tone for the people to follow, but they failed to do so. And, sad to say, the people copied their religious leaders. Because they had no discernment, they received the priests they deserved. That is what Hosea meant when he said, 'Like people, like priests' (4:9). Just as they were like each other in spiritual decline, 'so they will be like each other in receiving judgement'.

This is what had happened: the people had turned their backs upon God's ordained way of guidance. They knew, in their heart of hearts, that they should be obeying God's Word and seeking his direction in prayer. That was the reason why God had given them the law, including the Ten Commandments. That was also why God had laid down how they should approach him in worship—by means of obedient hearts and burnt offerings. Yet instead of doing these things, they did what the heathen around them were doing. They turned their backs upon their Saviour God and his ordained way of approach, and consulted a wooden idol instead.

The reason why they did this was selfish. They thought that the religion of their fathers was not exciting enough. They found that the solemn, pure worship of God did not gratify their physical desires. And they wanted to be like all the other nations; they did not want to be different from those who lived around them. They were just like their forefathers in the days of the judges. Even though God was their King, the people of that generation had cried out to Samuel to give them a king. The only reason they gave was the fact that all the other nations had kings (1 Samuel 8:5).

Jeremiah also had something serious to say about this kind of thinking. He wrote:

> Has a nation ever changed its gods?
> (Yet they are not gods at all.)
> But my people have exchanged their Glory
> for worthless idols.

He concludes,

> 'Be appalled at this, O heavens,
> and shudder with great horror,'
>
> declares the LORD.
> 'My people have committed two sins:
> They have forsaken me,
> the spring of living water,
> and have dug their own cisterns,
> broken cisterns that cannot hold water' (Jeremiah 2:11-13).

The people wanted titillation rather than something that demanded a spiritual response. That is why they were happy to leave their religion to the priests. They did not want to have to think for themselves. This is so foolish. Anyone who leaves his or her personal holiness to others is in spiritual danger. No religious leader can give you salvation. Pastors cannot even make anyone believe on the Lord Jesus Christ. All they can do is to point out the way.

In Hosea's day the religious leaders enjoyed their feasting, their consorting with prostitutes (religious ones or otherwise) and indulging in excesses of wine. However, none of these activities brought them any nearer to understanding the mind and will of the Lord. In fact, the way they were behaving took away their understanding (4:11).

This is incredible; these were the people of God. The Lord had done so much for them, and here they were actually turning away from him and his worship to serve other gods—in fact idols that were only made from pieces of wood. Jeremiah had some severe things to say about the people of his day who did the same thing. In an almost sarcastic way he records in his prophecy: 'They say to wood, "You are my father," and to stone, "You gave me birth."' God's conclusion was:

> They have turned their backs to me
>   and not their faces;
> yet when they are in trouble, they [selfishly] say,
>   'Come and save us!'

Then the Lord continues:

> Where then are the gods you made for yourselves?
>   Let them come if they can save you
>   when you are in trouble!
> For you have as many gods
>   as you have towns, O Judah   (Jeremiah 2:27-28).

Not only did the people consult wooden idols, they also used sticks as divining rods. Instead of seeking God's will through prayer and the principles contained in the Word of God, they resorted to doing what the heathen did. They threw a bunch of sticks into the air and then considered the significance of where they fell (cf. Ezekiel 21:21).

When I was a boy one of my aunts sometimes emptied the tea out of her cup and looked at the pattern made by the tea leaves in the bottom of it. She tried to see if they indicated anything significant. But Christians who look up their horoscopes in their newspapers are behaving just as foolishly as these ancient Israelites. Such things might seem 'a bit of fun', but believers who do this are incurring God's wrath in the same way as these people of Israel did.

They followed heathen worship (4:13–14)

They offered sacrifices on the tops of mountains and they did so because the heathen did the same thing. They thought that they were still worshipping Yahweh, but they were not going about it in God's prescribed way. Nor did they have hearts set on obeying the Lord. They went up the mountains because they thought that in this way they would be nearer to God. They forgot that they were near to God when they called upon him in the way he had laid down for them.

Many years earlier God had told them what they should do about these heathen altars. He had said, 'These are the decrees and laws you must be careful to follow in the land that the Lord, the God of your fathers, has given you to possess—as long as you live in the land. Destroy completely all the places on the high mountains and on the hills and under every spreading tree where the nations you are dispossessing worship their gods. Break down their altars, smash their sacred stones and burn their Asherah poles in the fire; cut down the idols of their gods and wipe out their names from those places. You must not worship the Lord your God in their way' (Deuteronomy 12:1–4).

In the days of Hosea, many years later, they were still ignoring what God had told them to do. Therefore God was going to punish them. In the prophecy of Jeremiah we read:

'Your wickedness will punish you;
    your backsliding will rebuke you.
Consider then and realize

> how evil and bitter it is for you
> when you forsake the LORD your God
> and have no awe of me,'
>
> > declares the LORD, the Lord Almighty.
>
> 'Long ago you broke off your yoke
> and tore off your bonds;
> you said, "I will not serve you!"
> Indeed, on every high hill
> and under every spreading tree
> you lay down as a prostitute'   (Jeremiah 2:19–20).

Their worship of God had taken on an earthy, lustful course. Sex had them in its grip. This was not sex as laid down by God. The only way acceptable to the Lord is sex between one man and one woman, who are married to each other. The conventions of this world tell us that we must not discriminate against homosexuals and lesbians, and that we must accept that, providing a couple are faithful to each other, it does not matter that they are cohabiting. However, if we know such people then we ought to be doing everything in our power to encourage them to obey God's Word.

The Israelites were not only obsessed by sex, as so many people in the world seem to be today, but God says that they were possessed of 'a spirit of prostitution' (4:12). The men consorted with harlots and sacrificed with shrine-prostitutes. They were much like the city of Corinth in the days of Paul. It was no wonder that such a spirit had invaded that young church—so much so that Paul had to write to them to complain that there was sexual immorality among them and that a man had his father's wife (1 Corinthians 5:1).

The Israelite men of Hosea's time thought that it was all right to mix their religion with a bit of sex. They liked to do this up in the mountains under the shade of the oak, poplar and terebinth trees (4:13). It was very pleasant up there, under the shade of the leaves. Also they thought that no one could see the way they were behaving. But they forgot that God can see everything. Nothing is hidden from his sight (Psalm 69:5). But when they found that their young women were doing the same thing, they were horrified. The women may have taken part because they did not want to miss out on the excitement! However, it may have been a kind of ritual in order 'to ensure fertility in their subsequent marriages'. Whatever the case, God's standards of behaviour and morality had been overturned. Any people who behave like this are 'without understanding' of God's will and 'will come to ruin!' Yet God would not condemn the women because the men were not setting a good example of holy living (4:14).

They were a bad example to others (4:15–19)

Judah, the southern kingdom, was far from perfect. Yet they were warned not to copy the ways of their northern neighbours, the Israelites. What a sad indictment it was that others had to be warned against the behaviour of those who were God's chosen ones! The people of Judah were told that if they were influenced by Israel then they, too, would be just as guilty—and therefore, under the punishment of the Almighty.

The Lord still pleaded with Israel. They were not to go up to Gilgal. There, years before, God had rolled away the disgrace of Egypt from his people (Joshua 5:9). In that place a monument had been set up to remind the Israelites of how God had saved them (Joshua 4:20). But by the time of Hosea Gilgal had become 'the centre of filthy "worship" to gods who had never redeemed anyone!'

The Israelites were also told not to go up to 'Beth Aven'. This was originally named Bethel—the house of God. It was the place where God first revealed himself to Jacob, and where, many years later, he renewed to Jacob the promises originally made to Abraham and gave him the name of Israel (Genesis 28:19; 35:9–14). However, Jeroboam 1 had later erected a shrine in this place, and one at Daniel He placed golden calves in each one so that the people could worship there (1 Kings 12:28-30). As a result of this idolatrous worship Bethel was now such a wicked place that God called it Beth Aven—'the house of iniquity'.

Despite all these warnings to refrain from places associated with idolatry, God knew the hearts of his people. He declared, 'The Israelites are stubborn, like a stubborn heifer.' The Lord actually wanted to bless his people. His desire was that they should be pastured like lambs in a meadow. He wanted them to experience the blessing David wrote about in the 23rd Psalm:

> The LORD is my shepherd, I shall not be in want.
>   He makes me lie down in green pastures,
> he leads me beside quiet waters,
>   he restores my soul.
> He guides me in paths of righteousness
>   for his name's sake.
> Even though I walk
>   through the valley of the shadow of death,
> I will fear no evil,
>   for you are with me;
> your rod and your staff,
>   they comfort me.
> You prepare a table before me
>   in the presence of my enemies.
> You anoint my head with oil;
>   my cup overflows.
> Surely goodness and love will follow me
>   all the days of my life,
> and I will dwell in the house of the LORD for ever.

But Israel was not prepared to yield to the ways of God. If she would not put herself in a position where she could be turned around, how could she be given the freedom of pasture?

The Lord concludes this passage by speaking about Israel's shame. Because this northern kingdom is 'joined [married] to idols', God's advice to everyone is to 'leave him alone' (4:17). These Israelites loved to lose their inhibitions and fear by drowning them in strong drink. They were like those concerning whom Micah prophesied: 'If a liar and deceiver comes and says, "I will prophesy for you plenty of wine and beer," he would be just the prophet for this people!' (Micah 2:11). But even when the drink ran out and they were left with a hangover, the Israelites still continued in their prostitution. They found excitement in indulging in sinful ways. However, God would not let them carry on like this for ever: 'A whirlwind will sweep them away, and their sacrifices will bring them shame.' In other words, the Assyrian hordes would swoop down on them like a whirlwind and take them away.

A call to genuine worship

We can easily condemn these people, but are we any better? We may not consort with prostitutes, give worship to false gods, or drown our sorrows in too much alcohol, yet we must make sure that we are not just going through the motions in our religion. We should seek the Lord from the heart. Our love for God must be real; it is too easy to have a sham religion that is undertaken merely to impress those around us, or even to fool ourselves into thinking that we are behaving in a godly way.

Our worship of the Lord must be genuine also. Worship is not just something which we undertake in church on Sundays; the whole of our lives should be given over to the honour and praise of our glorious God. It will do us no good if we merely pretend to worship the Lord. We actually have to come before him in humility and repentance and put him first and foremost in our own personal lives, in our church and community life.

Unlike the people of Israel, we should be aware of those around us. It is not good enough to say that we love God; we have to demonstrate to everyone that we have been changed by the wonder-working power of our gracious God and, as a result of our salvation, we are living for the benefit of others. We do not live in isolation; we should be godly examples to others. Paul said of the Corinthian believers, 'You yourselves are our letter, written on our hearts, known and read by everybody' (2 Corinthians 3:2). In our day we, too, should remember that we are being observed and 'read' by others.

8

How self-centred are you?

Please read Hosea 5:1–15

H ave you come across people who are so arrogant that you don't feel like telling them anything? They are pompous and they give the impression that they are the only ones who know anything worth knowing. Such people are not pleasant to know. We do not find ourselves drawn to them, and we certainly have no desire to count them among our friends. Yet that is exactly how God described the attitude of the inhabitants of the northern kingdom of Israel (5:5). They were so full of their own importance that they failed to understand that their problems were of their own making.

They seem to have argued like this: 'We are God's chosen people. We have our priests among us who perform their duties satisfactorily, and we have many places of worship scattered throughout our land. Therefore, no one can accuse us of failing to carry out our religious ceremonies on a regular basis. Unfortunately we have some among us who claim that we are not honouring God, but these people who call themselves prophets forget that we, as a nation, are the apple of God's eye.'

This is the danger for all who live in a land where the gospel has been preached for very many years. They would argue, 'This is a Christian land. We don't need to take notice of those who say we are in danger of God's judgement.'

That kind of thinking is so very foolish—especially for those of us who live in Britain. If we are spiritually sensitive then we have to admit that, as a nation, we have largely abandoned the faith of our fathers, and we are all in moral and spiritual danger. So very many of our country's laws, which were based on the Ten Commandments, have now been adjusted to take account of modern thinking. To make matters worse, many scholars in our theological colleges are teaching that talk about God's wrath against sin is nonsense and should be ignored.

Of course, it is true that we do not like to think about God's judgement against sin, on us or our land—any more than we want to contemplate our own death; but that does not mean that these things will not come to pass!

Now it may help us to put our own lives into proper perspective if we spend some time thinking about the attitude of the people of Israel (or Ephraim) in Hosea's day, and try to discover what God has to say to us about our own self-centred way of thinking.

They blamed others (5:1-4)

At the beginning of this chapter we see that God is still bringing his charges against the people. From Hosea 4:4 onwards the Lord has been concentrating on the waywardness of the priests, but now he broadens out his accusations as he addresses three groups of people. First of all, he speaks to the 'priests'. Secondly, he voices his concerns to the 'Israelites'; very likely this warning is directed mainly to the elders, but, ultimately, it would have included all the people. Finally God addresses the 'royal house', as well as the royal family themselves (5:1). This would have included all the administrative officials of the royal household.

God attracts their attention by saying, 'Hear this', 'Pay attention' and 'Listen'. When I was teaching in a secondary school I seem to remember using very similar words to urge my pupils to take notice of particularly important things that they needed to know. What was it that God wanted all these people (the whole nation of Israel) to concentrate upon? His concern was to make them think about the coming judgement, the matter that he had been speaking about at the end of chapter 4. He calls it 'this judgement'.

God's judgement was no light thing. It was going to be very severe. Throughout this chapter the Lord uses very many powerful adjectives to describe it. But the thing to notice here is that God tells them, 'This judgement is against you.' Although the punishment was going to be unleashed upon everyone, the main responsibility for its coming was laid at the feet of all the leaders of the people. The priests were still to take the largest share of the blame. However, anyone in a position of responsibility in the community was also guilty. This was because they saw the wickedness of the land but kept silent! God does not take kindly to those who are perceptive enough to realize that things are wrong, yet fail to do anything at all to warn people of the danger they are in.

These leaders were singled out because they were answerable to God for the state of the land. He says that they had been 'a snare' to the people. The picture that is used here is of someone trying to catch birds. Hosea was evidently referring to some specific events which have not come down to us in written documents, but it is obvious that the people would have known what he meant. What we are certain of is that Mizpah had once been a place of great religious significance. It was there that Samuel had begun his annual circuit for judging the people (see 1 Samuel 7:5–11,15–16). Bethel (called in this prophecy Beth Aven) and Gilgal were also on this yearly tour, and Tabor was a large, flat-topped mountain which still dominates the land to the south-west of the Sea of Galilee. From the top of this mountain can be seen, among other places, the village of Endor where there had once lived a witch (1 Samuel 28:7).

This is the charge: God accused the priests of trapping the people in these places. Just as a bird-hunter would have used snares and nets to catch his prey, so, whatever it was that they had done, God accuses them of deliberately setting out to deceive the very people they should have been helping to come to God. Moreover, they were not only leading the people astray from the truth; they were also encouraging them to live in immoral ways. In fact, the priests were behaving just like the woman of whom we read in Proverbs 7 that she came out on the street dressed like a prostitute, with the specific intention of meeting a simple young man who lacked judgement (Proverbs 7:7–23). He would have been easy prey for her. Her intention was to ensnare him for her own ends, and these would have been to his detriment. The prostitute's objectives were the acquisition of money and power and the enhancement of her own self-esteem. These are the same things that many Christian people long after today.

Hosea says that the priests of his day were deceiving the people in just the same kind of way. Just as God saw what was going on when they offered sacrifices on the tops of mountains (see 4:13), so he also knew all about the corruption of Ephraim. It was not, and could not be, hidden from his sight. God spoke through Jeremiah in a similar vein about unworthy priests:

'If they had stood in my council,
    they would have proclaimed my words to my people
and would have turned them from their evil ways
    and from their evil deeds.
Am I only a God nearby,'
    declares the LORD,
    'and not a God far away?
Can anyone hide in secret places
    so that I cannot see him?'
    declares the LORD.
'Do not I fill heaven and earth?'
    declares the LORD   (Jeremiah 23:22–24).

The same kind of thing was happening in Hosea's day, and all this evil had one big effect. It prevented the people from returning to God. They were guilty of sinful behaviour, but the problem was that they would not admit it. This is what so often causes people to stumble in our days. They know that they have sinned, but they are not prepared to confess it. The psalmist knew the folly of unconfessed sin. He said, 'If I had cherished sin in my heart, the Lord would not have listened [when I prayed]' (Psalm 66:18).

The reason why the people of Israel were unable to return to God was because they fostered within them a spirit of prostitution, rather than a hunger for true godliness. In other words, they sought for physical gratification rather than spiritual holiness.

Their arrogance prevented them from repenting (5:4–7,13)

Their pride caused them to stumble in their sin. They thought that they could disobey God's Word and still keep up their profession of godliness. But their evil ways tripped them up in their desire to walk in the paths of righteousness.

The person who thinks he can behave however he likes, because he is a Christian, is very foolish. Just because God has saved us for all eternity, that does not mean we can carry on sinning for all we are worth. Paul dealt with that way of thinking. He asked the question: 'Shall we go on sinning, so that grace may increase?' His prompt answer was: 'By no means! We died to sin; how can we live in it any longer?' (Romans 6:1–2).

Therefore, we see that the mark of a truly godly person is humility. But these people of Israel were far from that. They were arrogant; God tells them this (5:5). His Word declares, and human experience confirms, that 'Pride goes before destruction, a haughty spirit before a fall' (Proverbs 16:18).

These people were not only guilty of arrogance; they were reprehensible because they were displaying a pretence of religion. They made an outward attempt to seek the Lord. Certainly they took their flocks and herds to the altars of sacrifice, yet they did not find God there, and the reason was that he had withdrawn himself from them. The Lord was no longer at their traditional places of worship because they had desecrated these sites by their ungodly behaviour and children were born into their homes as a result of their heathen and immoral practices. They gave the impression that they were honouring God, but they were proving to be an offence to him. The reason was because they were unfaithful to him. They had given birth to illegitimate children, both spiritual children and also literal babies. And their New Moon festivals had been held in such an irreligious way that they were going to backfire upon the participants. Instead of bringing blessing to those who took part in them, these festivals were going to bring punishment upon the people and upon their fields.

The Baal fertility rites would not bring a prosperous harvest. Rather the people would face both spiritual and literal famine. It is the same for our land today. We have a great deal of pomp and religious ceremony in some of our churches and cathedrals, but we have to admit that in very many places there is famine. This is not a physical famine, but it is the kind of famine that Amos speaks about:

'The days are coming,' declares the Sovereign LORD,
  'when I will send a famine through the land—
not a famine of food or a thirst for water,
  but a famine of hearing the words of the LORD'

(Amos 8:11).

Certainly in Britain it is possible to listen to a church service on the radio and not hear the Word of God expounded.

When the people of Israel finally became aware of the danger they were in, they did seek help, but they looked in the wrong place. Instead of turning to the Lord their God, they turned to 'the great king' for help (5:13). This was the King of Assyria. They recognized their dire situation, but they went to the wrong person for assistance—even though he was called 'the great king'. In fact, it was this very king, and his nation of Assyria, that was to prove the downfall of the northern kingdom of Israel. In 2 Kings we read, 'Menahem son of Gadi became king of Israel, and he reigned in Samaria for ten years. He did evil in the eyes of the LORD. During his entire reign he did not turn away from the sins of Jeroboam son of Nebat, which he had caused Israel to commit. Then Pul king of Assyria invaded the land, and Menahem gave him a thousand talents of silver to gain his support and strengthen his own hold on the kingdom' (2 Kings 15:17–19). So, instead of providing help for Israel, Assyria became their undoing.

God dealt with their waywardness (5:8–12,14–15)
An alarm was sounded (5:8). Each of the three places mentioned

here, Gibeah, Ramah and Beth Aven, was on the border between Judah and Israel. They were all in the territory of Benjamin. Gibeah and Ramah were hilltop towns a few miles to the north of Jerusalem. From these towns people would see in the distance the approach of an invading army. In any case, the Assyrians were now a threat to both Israel and Judah. But God was also judging 'Judah's leaders'; the danger did not only come from outside the country. These leaders were 'like those who moved boundary stones'. Extending one's territory by stealing caused many neighbourhood disputes. This had been specifically condemned by God in Deuteronomy 19:14 and 27:17. But the people were not only doing this literally; they were also doing it in a spiritual sense. They had extended their borders of moral and spiritual behaviour. They 'removed the landmarks that distinguished between right and wrong'.

They may have thought that they were doing the wise thing, but God tells them what was actually going to happen. They had their ideas of what the enemy was likely to do, but God actually knows what will take place, and through his prophet Hosea he proclaims 'what is certain' (5:9). 'On the day of reckoning', Ephraim would be 'laid waste'.

God was going to 'pour out [his] wrath upon them'. This would come upon them 'like a flood of water' (5:10). Floods bring great destruction in their wake, and Israel would be flushed down the pan like so much worthless waste product. This punishment was going to come like a lion, 'like a great lion' who roars in his anger and tears animals and people to pieces (5:14). Like a lion, Assyria was preparing to pounce upon them and take them away to its lair, and there devour them. No one would come to their aid. History has told us some of the barbaric cruelty of the Assyrians. These things are too awful to describe here. Assyria is a picture of the devil who, like a roaring lion, prowls around looking for someone to devour (1 Peter 5:8).

But Israel's punishment would not only come upon them with great noise; it would also descend upon them quietly and slowly. Because Ephraim was so intent on pursuing idols, God was going to come upon them like a moth and like dry rot (5:12). Both of these things move almost imperceptibly, but they both do a great deal of damage as they eat into valuable materials. Jesus warned his disciples about moth and rust. He said, 'Do not store up for yourselves treasures on earth, where moth and rust destroy, and where thieves break in and steal' (Matthew 6:19). Instead we should be storing up treasures in heaven. And we do that by knowing and doing God's will.

God's final word in this chapter is, perhaps, the most devastating of all. He says, 'I will go back to my place' (5:15). He was going to leave them to their own devices. Paul spoke about this in his epistle to the Romans: 'God gave [those who behaved wickedly] over in the sinful desires of their hearts to sexual impurity for the degrading of their bodies with one another' (Romans 1:24). He left them so that they could have their own way. But they would also be a prey to great evil: 'They exchanged the truth of God for a lie, and worshipped and served created things rather than the Creator—who is for ever praised' (Romans 1:25). The reason he did this was so that they would admit their guilt, and in their misery earnestly seek God.

It is those things that our God graciously wants to bring us in our day. He has done so much in order to bring us to our senses. He even sent his own dear Son from heaven to die on the cruel cross to bear the punishment for our sins and redeem us, and yet we still want to persist in our own arrogant, selfish ways. When Jesus looked out over Jerusalem just before his arrest he said, 'O Jerusalem, Jerusalem, you who kill the prophets and stone those sent to you, how often I have longed to gather your children together, as a hen gathers her chicks under her wings ...' And then he utters those last few, sad words: 'but you were not willing' (Matthew 23:37).

How genuine is your repentance?

Please read Hosea 6:1–11

'I'm really sorry.' How often has someone said that to you, perhaps after breaking something which belonged to you? And in reply you have smiled sweetly and said, 'Don't worry. It doesn't really matter.' And you may have genuinely meant it because you have learned that life is too short to cry over spilt milk.

But how would you feel if the person who had wronged you, and apologized so eloquently, then went on to show no remorse at all, but instead continued to treat your property without due care, and generally to behave as though he didn't mean a word he said when he apologized so profusely? How would you feel then?

I wonder how many times Gomer apologized to Hosea for her immoral behaviour. I can imagine her coming up to him at bedtime and, with a coy look in her eyes, whispering in his ear, 'I'm so sorry, darling. Please forgive me. I don't know what I was thinking of in going after those other men. It won't happen again.'

Now, that is the kind of problem which faces us in this chapter as we look at Hosea 6. The Israelites started off by saying that they wanted to return to the Lord. But were they sincere in saying that they wanted to be back in a right relationship with their God?

We do not know whether verses 1–3 are being spoken by the Israelites, or whether they are words that Hosea used to indicate what they were thinking. Whatever the case, we can be certain of one thing.

Israel took notice of God's Word (6:1–3)

At the close of chapter 5 God had pronounced judgement on the northern kingdom. He had told them that Assyria would descend on them and tear them to pieces like a fierce lion, and they would be cruelly taken away to the lion's lair (5:14). God would leave them there in the clutches of their enemy. The reason why the Lord was going to allow these things to happen was to bring his people to their senses. He wanted them to admit their guilt and seek his face and his forgiveness (5:15).

In the opening verses of this section we see the people apparently seeking a proper return to the Lord. They said to each other, 'Come, let us return to the Lord.' In using the word 'return', they were admitting that they were drifting away from God; otherwise they would not have said that they wanted to go back to him. They admitted that they were in a dire situation. They acknowledged that it was the Lord who had torn them to pieces and had injured them (see also 5:13). But they also realized that they were, in some sense, dead.

Did they mean that they were dead spiritually? Whatever they felt, they knew that they needed to be revived so that they could 'live in his presence' once again. How genuine was their sorrow? It appears that there was a degree of sincerity in their words because they believed that this 'deadness' would only last for a comparatively short while. That is why they said, 'After two days he will revive us; on the third day he will restore us.'

The mention of 'the third day' has led many to think that this verse is referring to the resurrection of the Lord Jesus Christ on 'the third day'. On the road to Emmaus Jesus told two of his puzzled disciples, 'This is what is written: The Christ will suffer and rise from the dead *on the third day*' (Luke 24:46). This verse may also have been one of the scriptures that Paul had in mind when he wrote, 'For what I received I passed on to you as of first importance: that Christ died for our sins according to the Scriptures, that he was buried, that he was raised *on the third day* according to the Scriptures' (1 Corinthians 15:3–4). However, we need to be cautious here. Although the only Old Testament reference to a third-day resurrection is here in Hosea 6:1–2, it is clear that this verse has much more to do with the restoration of *Israel* (being revived after 'two days'). Hosea 6:2 is clearly teaching that (in the Messiah) Israel had been redeemed.

Therefore, we must be careful if we are thinking that this verse points towards Christ's resurrection on the third day, because the whole context refers to those who have gone astray from God's paths. What is recorded here in Hosea is more in line with the words of Romans 6:3–4: 'Don't you know that all of us who were baptized into Christ Jesus were baptized into his death? We were therefore buried with him through baptism into death in order that, just as Christ was raised from the dead through the glory of the Father, we too may live a new life.' This section is about being brought to spiritual life.

We can see, then, that these opening words of chapter 6 appear to express a desire on the part of the people to return to God and his ways. However, when we move on to verse 4 we find that there seems to be a lack of *true* repentance about them. Two factors are missing: there is no real confession of their sin, and there is an absence of any serious promise of any moral change in their behaviour. We are reminded of the words of Catherine the Great, who said of God, 'The good Lord will pardon; that's his trade.' The people appear to be just taking it for granted that if they return to God, then he will say, 'Welcome back. Never mind about your sin. It doesn't matter.' But that is not what the Word of God teaches us. Our sin *does* matter. It causes such offence that the Lord Jesus Christ had to go all the way to the cross to die for sinners, so that they might be forgiven and cleansed.

On the other hand, the Israelites were certain of some things. They knew that although God had injured them, he was the one who could bind up their wounds, revive them and restore them. They were conscious too, of certain obligations which they needed to undertake. They were required to 'acknowledge the LORD', and they knew that they needed to 'press on to acknowledge him'. The necessity of knowing God and acknowledging him is seen over and over again in Hosea's prophecy. A person who has no personal acquaintance with God is in a sad position. However, knowing God is not something that just happens when we perform religious ceremonials. Knowing God comes about through much effort and determination on our part. It is also very true that without exercising faith in the Lord Jesus Christ no one can know the Lord or enjoy his presence; without faith it is impossible to please him (Hebrews 11:6).

Knowing God was only the first step on the way back to God for these Israelites; they were also required to acknowledge him—before everyone. They were obliged to be open about their faith. It was necessary that they should be unashamed about their knowledge of God. We, today, as believers in the Lord Jesus Christ, should live with this same sentiment. As Isaac Watts put it:

I'm not ashamed to own my Lord
Or to defend his cause,
Maintain the honour of his Word,
The glory of his cross.

That is why new believers desire to be baptized. They want to declare their faith in Christ alone to everyone.

Finally, the Israelites knew that God always kept his word. He was like his own creation, the sun. Every morning, since the Lord created it, the sun has risen and set out on its daily course (except on the occasion recorded in Joshua 10:12-14, when the sun stood still for one whole day). The sun will continue to rise and set each day until the end of time. In the same way, God's people can be certain that when the Lord comes back to his people he will shower his blessings upon them. Living in the presence of God will be like basking in the warmth of the sun. It will be like drinking in refreshing rain that brings fertility to the parched earth.

That figure is somewhat lost on those of us who live in Britain. We do not find winter rain refreshing, but for the Israelites, when the rain fell on their dry and barren land it spoke to them of a rich harvest. The psalmist expresses these feelings like this: 'You have made known to me the path of life; you will fill me with joy in your presence, with eternal pleasures at your right hand' (Psalm 16:11).

God was exasperated with them (6:4–6)
In speaking of God in this way we are using a human expression which cannot properly be applied to God, any more than we

can speak of the strength which is in his arm, or of the guidance which he gives with his eye.

We have seen that the Israelites expressed their desire to return to the Lord. They openly acknowledged that no one else could revive them. They were aware, too, of their obligations to God. In these opening verses of Hosea 6 they were expressing similar thoughts to those contained in the very last chapter of this prophecy. In that passage we read that their God was going to reply to their cry like this: 'I will heal their waywardness and love them freely' (14:4).

Why, then, does the Lord say, 'What can I do with you, Ephraim? What can I do with you, Judah? Your love is like the morning mist, like the early dew'? (6:4). Why does God appear to pour cold water on their words when they say they will return to the Lord? In this verse he is saying to them, 'Your profession of love to me only lasts for a brief while. It is like the mist of an early summer morning, which, as soon as the sun rises and shines upon it, disappears.' In other words, God assessed their repentance and found it superficial. He knew that as soon as trouble came upon them their professed faithfulness to God and his Word would wither away. Their professed desire to return to God was worth no more than the words of the Israelites to which the psalmist refers when he says:

> Whenever God slew them, they would seek him;
>   they eagerly turned to him again ...
> But then they would flatter him with their mouths,
>   lying to him with their tongues;
> their hearts were not loyal to him,
>   they were not faithful to his covenant (Psalm 78:34,36–37).

So, as Hosea spoke these words to the people, he must have felt an echo of them in his own heart. God was crying out to

Ephraim, and also to Judah, 'What can I do with you?' How often Hosea must have uttered similar words to Gomer! I imagine that there were occasions when Gomer had cried her eyes out in sorrow as she pledged her undying love to Hosea and assured him that she would never be unfaithful to him again. But her promise had only lasted until she saw the next handsome man making eyes at her. And then she had turned her back upon her husband, leaving him heartbroken and ashamed. We can almost hear him crying out, 'What can I do with you, Gomer? Why are you so unfaithful to me? And why, oh why, do you keep saying that you will give up your philandering—and then break your word the very next minute?'

The 'loyalty' of the Israelites had been just as fleeting as that of Gomer. God had sent his prophets to the people, but they had ignored what these prophets said, and had dealt with them very badly. Elijah, Elisha and Amos had all been treated with contempt. That was why God was going to 'cut [the Israelites] to pieces' with his words. His judgements were going to flash upon them 'like lightning' (6:5).

Jesus told a parable about this in Luke 20:9–16. It is the story of a man who owned a vineyard. He let it out to tenant farmers, but every time he sent a servant to collect some of the harvest the tenants treated the man very badly and sent him away empty-handed. God's people are called his vineyard (see Isaiah 5:1–7). But every time the Lord sent one of his prophets to collect what was due to him (i.e. love and loyalty), the people of the land treated God's servants shamefully. And so, because of this, God was going to punish them very severely.

It is quite clear to us that the Israelites were insincere in their profession of repentance. They thought that they could keep God on their side by offering him sacrifices and burnt offerings. However, he said again here what he said in so many other places, 'I desire mercy, not sacrifice, and acknowledgement of God rather than burnt offerings' (6:6; cf. Matt 9:13; 12:7; 1 Samuel 15:22–23; Isaiah 1:12–17; Amos 5:21–24; Micah 6:6–8). In other words, 'Sacrifice apart from faithfulness to the Lord's will is wholly unacceptable to him.'

Israel's actions would condemn them (6:7–11)
This last section of the chapter is once again filled with a catalogue of unfaithfulness. Just as Gomer had broken her marriage bond with her husband, Hosea, so the Israelites had been unfaithful to their God. They had broken the covenant God had made with them.

The words, 'like Adam' (6:7), may be a reference to the breaking of God's commandment not to eat of the tree which was in the middle of the Garden of Eden. Or Hosea may have meant the town named Adam (see Joshua 3:16) and some terrible crime that had taken place there.

'Gilead', too, had turned into a place of blood. The men of Gilead had been involved in the murder of King Pekahiah (2 Kings 15:25). One commentator tells us, 'The road from Samaria to Bethel, the chief seat of the calf worship, led through Shechem, and pilgrims coming from or going to Bethel were murdered, raped, outraged by gangs of priests.' Of this atrocious and bloodthirsty behaviour the Lord says, 'I have seen a horrible thing in the house of Israel' (6:10). This verse is God's assessment of Israel's behaviour. Like Gomer, Israel had not only cast aside her marriage vows, she had also given herself up to prostitution, 'taking up with any customer—any pagan deity or cultic novelty—that comes along'.

The result of all this was that God appointed a harvest when the people would reap what they had sown. In other words, it would be a time of God's judgement when anything that was of use would be saved, but everything that was unworthy would be burnt up in the fires of destruction. This harvest was not just for the northern kingdom. God said, 'Also for you, Judah, a harvest is appointed' (6:11). Judah was going to have to wait for over another century before she was to reap the reward of her evil-doing. But for Israel the lion (of Assyria) was already waiting to pounce!

It may be thought that the Israelites had made clear their desire to repent in the opening verses of this chapter. Certainly those words sound very good and they were all the correct things to say: the people acknowledged that it was God who had wounded them, they believed that he could heal them and they knew that God was faithful to his word. However, there was something missing in their confession. They did not admit their guilt. 'They have faced their woundedness (v.2; cf. 5:12-13) but not their waywardness. Healing is sought, even resurrection, but no specific sin in mentioned.' This is what God had required them to do in 5:15, but there is not a hint of their admission of sin; that was where they went wrong.

We need to ensure that we are not as insincere in our profession of repentance. Sinners need to recognize that they can do nothing towards their salvation except cast themselves upon the Lord. This is the very thing that Israel failed to do, and severe and permanent judgement came upon them (for they never survived their captivity in Assyria—not as a nation, anyway).

How different was David's prayer in Psalm 51! There he cried:

Have mercy on me, O God,
    according to your unfailing love;
according to your great compassion
    blot out my transgressions.

Wash away all my iniquity
    and cleanse me from my sin.
For I know my transgressions,
    and my sin is always before me.
Against you, you only, have I sinned
    and done what is evil in your sight ...
Surely I was sinful at birth,
    sinful from the time my mother conceived me ...
Cleanse me with hyssop, and I shall be clean;
    wash me, and I shall be whiter than snow ...
Hide your face from my sins
    and blot out all my iniquity.
Create in me a pure heart, O God,
    and renew a steadfast spirit within me
                     (Psalm 51:1–10; cf. 13–14).

That is the kind of confession that God wants to hear. It is for such sinners that Christ went all the way to the cross and shed his precious cleansing blood to pay the price for their sin.

10

A cookery lesson

Please read Hosea 6:11–7:10

Many people over the age of fifty can recall what they were doing when President Kennedy was assassinated. I was at a prayer meeting on that Friday evening. But here is a question that takes us back even further: can you remember what you were doing on the day Queen Elizabeth II was crowned? I can. For the first part of the morning I watched some workmen taking out an old kitchen range and installing a new living-room open fire in its place. Later on I went to my aunt's house to watch the coronation ceremony on her nine-inch black-and-white television—little dreaming that one day I would interview on the radio the bishop who stood on her left-hand side at the moment when the crown was placed on her head.

My mother was very pleased that her old 'kitchener' had been removed. She hated it because she had to get up early to chop the wood for it. Then she had to light the fire and wait for a long time until the oven was hot enough to cook with. It had no temperature controls; she just had to judge when the oven was at the correct temperature for the particular food she wanted to cook.

Ovens were a little like that in the time of Hosea. They were usually made of clay and built with a flat stone bottom, on which the fire was lit. This heated up the whole oven, including the walls. These walls sloped upwards towards an opening left at the top of the oven. As the fire burned, so the flames shot up until they emerged through the hole at the top.

In this section of Hosea our eyes are drawn to a kitchen, and particularly to an oven. We have a picture of the baker kneading his dough and then letting it rise (7:4). We see the oven, having been lit the day before, left to smoulder all night. Then in the morning we see its flames leaping up as the baker stirs them up again (7:6).

When we come to verse 8 we find another image taken from cookery. On this occasion the picture is of some flat cakes of bread which, unfortunately, had been burnt black on one side but left uncooked and soggy on the other. This was because the baker had forgotten to turn the cake over halfway through the cooking.

The message of these verses concerns Israel and their religious leaders. They are seen as raging like a flaming oven, and the people of God are described as being like a half-baked cake. The people were in a sad state (7:1). Every time God opened up the way for them to return to him and his ways, the cracks began to show. The sins of the people were exposed; God called these sins 'crimes'. God took note of everything that was happening in the land (7:2). It was foolish of the people to behave like this because God had declared many times that he could see everything. For example, the psalmist said, 'You [God] have set our iniquities before you, our secret sins in the light of your presence' (Psalm 90:8). Just as the Israelites were foolish not to realize that God was watching their evil deeds, so we today are foolish if we forget that God sees everything we do.

Even though the leaders of Israel and the people had given some small show of repentance, God declared that this was really deceit (7:1). Fine-sounding words of sorrow had been used at the beginning of chapter 6, but we have seen that, without a confession of guilt, these were in fact worth nothing. They were empty, and so they were deceitful. The sad fact was that there was very much evil taking place, yet no one had any concern about the social conditions of the people. 'Thieves break into houses, bandits rob in the streets' (7:1). Yet they were all so steeped in sin that they were engulfed in it, and were not convicted of their evil ways.

They forgot that God sees everything. Nothing is hidden from his sight. The prodigal son came to a point in his life when he realized that he had sinned against heaven and against his father (Luke 15:18). But the people had no understanding of the seriousness of their behaviour. God does have, however, and he summed up their action as adultery (7:4). He said they are 'all adulterers'.

What does the Bible say about adultery? Deuteronomy 22:22 tells us that if a man is found lying with a married woman, both shall die. God views adultery as something which is very sinful, and a matter which must be dealt severely. In John 8:3 we read that the teachers of the law and the Pharisees brought before Jesus a woman caught in adultery and they reminded him that the law of Moses commanded that such a person was to be stoned to death.

So what does God mean when here, in Hosea 7:4, he calls the Israelites adulterers? He is saying that, like Hosea's wife, they had been unfaithful in turning away from their own God and turning towards other gods. In this case the gods towards which they had turned were not Baal, but the gods of 'power', 'prestige' and 'authority'.

The leaders of the people were burning with lust (7:3-7)
Hosea says that they were 'burning like an oven' (7:4). The people listening to Hosea would have known that an oven was often lit the night before cooking was to take place. When the fire was alight it would be damped down and left to smoulder all night. This meant that it would be gradually, but slowly, heating up the oven during all this period, although nothing spectacular would be seen by anyone looking on.

That is what the hearts of the leaders were like. All the while that they were giving the impression that they were wanting to please the king, they were plotting to overthrow him (7:3). They fed the king's mind with wicked thoughts. They told his sons lies. All of this would have lulled the king into a false sense of security.

Next we have a picture of a great festival taking place (7:5). We are not told the reason for the celebration, but it may have been a party arranged for the birthday of the king. Whatever the case, we are told this: the wine flowed freely—so much so that the princes became inflamed with drink.

While the Bible does not condemn the actual consumption of alcohol, it most certainly does give us some very severe warnings about its dangers. Proverbs 23:31 tells us, 'Do not gaze at wine when it is red, when it sparkles in the cup, when it goes down smoothly! And the following verse continues: 'In the end it bites like a snake and poisons like a viper.' So, while the drinking of alcohol is not condemned, drunkenness most certainly is. This means that alcohol is a dangerous substance.

Here, at the king's party, we see that it was the princes who were rolling drunk. We cannot help wondering whether, if the king had set a better example to his children, they would not have behaved so foolishly. This incident is a solemn warning to all parents. We, ourselves, may exercise moderation in our use of drink, but how does our drinking affect the minds of our children (and our weaker brothers and sisters)? These people may not be so careful as we are ourselves in using alcohol. 1 Corinthians 8:9–13 sets out some of the principles involved here.

Because of all the wild partying, the king 'joins hands with the mockers' (7:5). We do not know who the mockers referred to in this verse were, but by saying that the king joined hands with them Hosea may mean that the king stretched out his hand in a toast to Baal, or to some other heathen god. Or he may have joined hands with those leaders who had been trying to ingratiate themselves with him.

Whatever the case, people who are rolling drunk do some very foolish things. Isaiah talks about Ephraim's drunkards (Isaiah 28:1). He goes on to describe the stupidity of those who indulge in too much wine. He tells us:

> [They] stagger from wine
>   and reel from beer:
> priests and prophets stagger from beer
>   and are befuddled with wine;
> they reel from beer,
>   they stagger when seeing visions,
>   they stumble when rendering decisions.

Then he gives this revolting description (which ought to put all of us off unwise indulgence in alcohol):

> All the tables are covered with vomit
> and there is not a spot without filth   (Isaiah 28:7–8).

While the king was getting drunk, the leaders of the people were planning his downfall. Hosea tells us, 'Their hearts are like an oven; they approach him with intrigue. Their passion smoulders all night' (7:6). Then, in the morning, when they are ready to do their foul deed, we see that their hearts blaze into a 'flaming fire'.

Fire is used to describe all kinds of human emotions. Like water, it can be man's best friend, or his worst enemy. We talk of a person being 'fired up' about some idea. We speak about having a burning desire, or being aflame with passion. But sometimes we burn with anger.

This is the picture before us. The leaders had been silently smouldering like an oven all night: 'All of them are hot as an oven; they devour their rulers.' The result is that 'Their kings fall' (7:7). During the last thirty years of Israel's existence six men reigned over the nation. 2 Kings 15 tells us about the shameful ways of most of these Israelite kings. Four of them killed their predecessors and then reigned in their places (2 Kings 15:10,14,25,30). The sad thing is that God says of these rulers, 'None of them calls on me.' When that happens to the leaders, the people are going to end up in a very sad condition. These men were supposed to be the leaders of God's people. Yet not only did they do their own thing; they all, with hardly an exception, failed to call upon their God. Geoffrey Treasure said, 'A prayerless Christian should be a non-existent species.' And in the nineteenth century C. H. Spurgeon wrote, 'We shall never see much change for the better in our churches in general till the prayer meeting occupies a higher place in the esteem of Christians.'

The people were foolish (7:8–10)

As we come to the next section we see that the theme of cooking continues. Hosea says, 'Ephraim is a flat cake not turned over.' When I grill veggie burgers I sometimes forget to turn them over after a few minutes. As a consequence, when I go back to the cooker I find that they have burned and that the side facing the glowing element has turned black. So, when I discover them like that, I turn them over and try to cook them just a little on the other side. When I serve them up to my vegetarian daughter I make sure that I place that lighter side upwards on the plate!

The picture here in verse 8 is of a flat cake of bread which is being cooked, but has been left in the oven for too long. When it is taken out the cook discovers that he or she has a cake which has burned to a cinder on one side, but the other side is all soft and soggy! In other words, this cake looks so unappetizing that no one would willingly want to consume it! That was how God saw the northern kingdom of Israel. One of my dictionaries says that half-baked means 'foolish or stupid' (Collins); in other words, God was saying that his people were worthless. My other dictionary says this word means 'half-witted', or 'not in earnest' (Oxford).

Why did God call Ephraim (that is, Israel) half-baked? We can see at least three reasons.

1. They mixed with the nations (7:8)

God had continually called on his people to be separate from all other peoples. That is what the word 'holy' means. However, in the days of the Exodus we find that the Israelites often grumbled about their leaders and about their God. In Exodus 16, for example, they are continually complaining. One of the reasons for this was that they had a mixed multitude travelling with them (see Exodus 12:38). Later on, when we come to the time of the judges, we see that they wanted to be like all the other nations which were around them (1 Samuel 8:5). God had warned them that this would be a recipe for disaster. If they copied the other nations they would begin to drift away from the Lord and matters would go badly for them.

It can be the same for us. Although we are required to be a witness in the world, we must always remember that we do not belong to the world; and therefore we should not live by a worldly system of thinking and behaviour. 2 Corinthians 6:14–18 tells us that we should come out from those who are not Christians. We should 'be separate' from all those who love the world and do not love God (see 1 John 2:15–17).

2. Foreigners had sapped their strength (7:9)
They had turned to Assyria for help. In fact, they had paid tribute to the Assyrians. This was not only sapping them politically and economically; it was also dragging them down spiritually and making them ineffective.

3. They were going mouldy (7:9)
It is said of Ephraim in this verse that 'His hair is sprinkled with grey'—and he had not noticed this deterioration. The mention of his hair being sprinkled with grey does not appear to refer in this instance to the ageing process. Here it means that grey, fuzzy mould was growing on him. Elsewhere in the Old Testament grey hair is always a sign of dignity and wisdom, but in this verse it is an indication of arrogance and failure to return to the Lord. Just like the moth and rot of 5:12, this mould was creeping over the Israelites and attacking them unawares. In the same way that we are unaware that last week's cakes have gone mouldy in the cake-tin, so they did not realize that God

saw them as only fit for destruction, even though their sins were testifying against them.

The need for heartfelt repentance

Whenever the Lord went to restore the fortunes of his people he only found iniquity exposed for all to see. Very sad to say, Israel still did not return to the Lord. Nor did they try to seek for him. This shows us the awful state the northern kingdom was in. We know from elsewhere in the Bible that God's fire of judgement is waiting to be unleashed against all wickedness. He is a consuming fire who will burn up all wickedness (see Hebrews 12:29). Even so, he says to sinful men and women, 'You will seek me and find me when you seek me with all your heart' (Jeremiah 29:13).

However, Israel did not return, or search for him. Why was that? It was because they refused to admit their guilt, or come in humble repentance to the Lord.

We are no better than the people of Israel in the time of Hosea. We have turned our backs on the Lord. We have gone our own way. We have wandered and strayed from God's paths like lost sheep. If only we will confess our sin and repent of it wholeheartedly then God will receive us. Yet, as we saw earlier when looking at the opening verses of Hosea 6, our repentance must be true and sincere. We do not deserve his mercy, but he has sent the Lord Jesus Christ to bring deliverance for people who are genuine in their desire to forsake sin and turn to the Lord in authentic love and faith.

11

A flying lesson

Please read Hosea 7:11–16

I passed my driving test the first time, but only after I had had a number of lessons. Most people find that driving a car is not as easy as they thought it was going to be. They go in for their first test feeling fairly confident, but to their great disappointment they fail. As I have been driving for some thirty-five years now, I do not find it too daunting to get behind the steering wheel and drive off. However, if I had to fly an aircraft, then it would be a different matter entirely. There is so much more to flying. If you are driving a car and get into trouble, or lose your way, all you have to do is draw in at the side of the road and try to sort out the problem. But if you are flying a plane you cannot merely draw into the side of the air-space. You have to land the plane first.

We have in this second half of Hosea 7 two pictures which have to do with flying. In the first one Ephraim (the northern kingdom of Israel) is compared to a dove, and in the second to a bow (the kind used for shooting arrows).

The kingdom was insecure (7:11–14)

God said that Ephraim was 'like a dove'. We always think of doves as symbols of peace. It was a dove which returned to Noah's ark with a freshly plucked olive leave in its beak (Genesis 8:11). The psalmist cried out, 'Oh, that I had the wings of a dove! I would fly away and be at rest' (Psalm 55:6). And in Jeremiah the dove is depicted as one of the birds that are sensible and obedient to God:

> Even the stork in the sky
>   knows her appointed seasons,
> and the dove, the swift and the thrush
>   observe the time of their migration   (Jeremiah 8:7).

Here, however, the dove is seen as a bird that is 'easily deceived and senseless'. When we looked at Hosea 7:9, we noticed that in that verse grey hair was not a symbol of wisdom, but one of mouldiness—so here the picture is the opposite of the one we normally associate with a dove.

Ephraim was 'like a dove' because the people had no heart. God uses similar language to describe his people in Jeremiah 5:21: 'Hear this, you foolish and senseless people, who have eyes but do not see, who have ears but do not hear.' These people, who had self-seeking religious leaders over them, did not know where to go. Therefore, they were easily deceived.

There was one small thing in their favour: at least they had reached the point where they knew that they were in real trouble. However, instead of going to the Lord, as they should have done, they flitted from place to place, just like silly birds. They flocked together (7:12) united in encouraging each other in their stupid ways. Similarly, in Isaiah 41:7 we read that:

The craftsman encourages the goldsmith,
>   and he who smooths with the hammer
>   spurs on him who strikes the anvil.
He says of the welding, 'It is good.'

These workmen were not encouraging each other in good works because the passage continues: 'He nails down the idol so that it will not topple.' In other words, they were encouraging each other in foolish idolatry. The people of Israel behaved like this because they did not know what to do for the best. So many of their kings had fallen, but none of them called on the Lord (see 7:7).

When any believer is in trouble he, or she, should seek the Lord. God is concerned about the welfare of his people and he has promised to guide them. He said:

I will lead the blind by ways they have not known,
>   along unfamiliar paths I will guide them;
I will turn the darkness into light before them
>   and make the rough places smooth.
These are the things I will do;
>   I will not forsake them   (Isaiah 42:16).

This means that, whatever happens to them:

God has said:
'Never will I leave you;
>   never will I forsake you.'
So we say with confidence, 'The Lord is my helper; I will not be afraid.
>   What can man do to me?'   (Hebrews 13:5–6).

If we have difficult decisions to make and we are in a dilemma, not knowing what to do, we must not flit from place to place looking for guidance. God tells us:

[When] the poor and needy search for water,
  but there is none;
  their tongues are parched with thirst.
... I the LORD will answer them;
  I, the God of Israel, will not forsake them   (Isaiah 41:17).

Ephraim did not do this; instead they called to Egypt and turned to Assyria. The history of the northern kingdom of Israel illustrates this frantic uncertainty. We find an example of this in 2 Kings 15:17–31 and 17:1–6. Kidner summarizes the sequence of events like this: 'King Menahem bought Assyria's patronage. His son's assassin, Pekah, went back on this alignment as soon as it ceased to suit him and lost half his kingdom. His successor, Hoshea, followed his example and lost the rest, for after renewing the allegiance he broke it by intrigue with Egypt, only to lose what little remained of his realm for ever.'

God was not prepared to let them get away with such foolish and evil behaviour. He observed them as they flew from place to place and as they congregated together, and he planned to act against them, as any farmer would do to combat troublesome birds. He was going to take a large net and throw it over them. He was going to 'pull them down like birds of the air'. Even though the Ephraimites had treated their God so badly, he did not fail to warn them of their dire situation. Through Hosea he calls:

Woe to them
  because they have strayed from me!
Destruction to them,
  because they have rebelled against me!

Just as Gomer had turned away from her husband, Hosea, so the people of Ephraim had not only strayed from their God, but had actually rebelled against him and spoken lies against him. Despite all their ingratitude towards their gracious God, the Lord still wanted them to return to him. He longed to redeem them. This word 'redeem' means 'buy back'. The Lord had redeemed their forefathers from slavery in Egypt, and still he wanted them to return to him. He was prepared to pay the cost. In Egypt the price was the death of a spotless lamb whose blood was shed. The price that God has paid to redeem sinners is the death of his own dear Son, the Lord Jesus Christ, on the cross of Calvary. Peter tells us, 'For you know that it was not with perishable things such as silver or gold that you were redeemed from the empty way of life handed down to you from your forefathers, but with the precious blood of Christ, a lamb without blemish or defect' (1 Peter 1:18–19).

When the people of Hosea's day became aware of the danger they were in, they cried out in a form of repentance—just as they had done in 6:1–3. They were cast down in despair. 'They ... wail upon their beds' (7:14). They recognized the awful situation they were in and they wanted someone to rescue them!

God wants us to come to him with tears of repentance. He longs for us to be truly sorry for all the wrong we have done in our lives. But his desire is that our tears should be genuine. He does not want us to cry in the way little children sometimes do, solely to get the sympathy of their mothers or teachers. He does not want us to tell him lies.

However, the tears that the people of Ephraim were shedding were like those of the priests of Baal on Mount Carmel. When the fire failed to come down on their sacrifice, 'They shouted louder and slashed themselves with swords and spears, as was their custom, until their blood flowed' (1 Kings 18:28).

The Israelites of Hosea's day were employing the same kind of tactics in their worship. They wailed upon their beds. This was where their priorities lay. Perhaps their beds reminded them of their 'worship' with their ritual prostitutes on the mountain-tops (see 4:13). Despite their feigned sorrow, they did not cry out to God because of their sin. They were far more concerned with their grain and new wine. One commentator says that their attitude was: 'Never mind about "Thy kingdom come"—where's our daily bread?' Another says, 'They were not interested in coming under the direction of God; they simply wanted an easier life and better harvests.'

Following this, at the end of verse 14 we read these very sad words: 'But [they] turn away from me.' They will turn to everything, and everyone, else, but not to their God who loves them and wants to redeem them. They were just like Gomer, who turned away from Hosea (who truly loved her) and turned instead to other lovers (who merely gave her a passing thrill). The pleasures of sin only last for a little while (Hebrews 11:25).

The whole of Israel was off course (7:15–16)

God had not only set this people apart for himself and for his glory, he had also 'trained them and strengthened them' (7:15). However, they treated his love with contempt. They had behaved towards their earthly kings with disrespect. Their attitude to their God was the same. The Lord explains, through his prophet: 'They plot evil against me.' They did so by not turning to the Most High. All they wanted was their own way. Little did they realize that 'There is a way that seems right to a man, but in the end it leads to death' (Proverbs 14:12).

The Ephraimites turned in every direction they could think of, but not towards their gracious and kind God. They called to Egypt, forgetting that God had called them *out* of that country, with its ungodliness and slavery. They also turned to Assyria, not realizing that this country was going to be their downfall! In addition, they looked upwards to the mountain-top shrines. But when they did so, they were not looking to the Most High; they sought only Baal and similar false gods.

It is for this reason that God calls Ephraim 'a faulty bow'. The people were in great danger and they knew that they needed to have an efficient army if they were going to be able to defend themselves. Yet God says to them, 'Your weapons are defective.' He speaks about their foolish past in Psalm 78:

> ... they put God to the test
> > and rebelled against the Most High;
> > they did not keep his statutes.
> Like their fathers they were disloyal and faithless;
> > as unreliable as a faulty bow.
> They angered [the Lord] with their high places;
> > they aroused his jealousy with their idols.
> When God heard them, he was very angry;
> > he rejected Israel completely　　　　　(Psalm 78:56–59).

Spiritually they were like a bow which could not shoot arrows accurately. In other words, they were ineffective in their fight against evil. This was because they were like bows which had loose strings. They had no power, nor did they have any speed in their attack. If they hit anything at all, it was not their enemy. Everything about them was totally sluggish!

Are God's people today any better? The Lord tells us that we are in a spiritual battle against sin, this world and the devil. To fight against these evils we need to be efficient. We are to be strong in the Lord and in his mighty power. For that to be the case we must 'put on the full armour of God' (Ephesians 6:11). We do that by having a regular and powerful prayer-life and by frequently studying the Word of God. If we fail to maintain our lives spiritually then we shall be slow to serve God—and we shall fail to hit the target we ought to be aiming at—which is not other Christians!

Because the people of Ephraim were slow to serve God and swift to do evil, Hosea tells them that terrible trouble was about to come upon them. Their leaders were going to fall by the sword. In a battle enemies could only get near enough to fight hand-to-hand with a sword if the archers had failed to keep them at a distance. The way in which Ephraim had been behaving had given their opponents the opportunity to get near to them. Their compromise with other nations had allowed this to happen. Their insolent, or arrogant, attitude towards God and his law had lulled them into a false sense of security. And their turning away from the Most High had left the way open for their opponents to creep up on them unawares.

When the time came for them to be defeated by the Assyrians they were going to be ridiculed in far-off lands. When Moses was leading the people through the desert he pleaded with God not to allow them to be defeated. However, here Hosea says that their descendants, the people of Ephraim, will not only be defeated, but destroyed because of their rebellion against God (7:13).

This chapter ends with the word 'Egypt'. It would have caused Hosea's hearers great consternation to look back on those 400 awful years of slavery that their forefathers had endured in Egypt. God tells Ephraim that what Moses had feared would happen to the Israelites whom he led was most certainly going to come to pass for the people of this generation. Because of their defeat they would 'be ridiculed in the land of Egypt' (7:16). They would find they had reverted to their old situation. The Israelites had certainly gone back on their word and returned to their evil ways. And they ought to be thoroughly ashamed of themselves!

We are in a similar situation today

So many people are looking for direction in these days. They seek it in drugs, cigarettes and alcohol. But none of these things will give them lasting satisfaction. Even huge wealth does not bring happiness, any more than it can guarantee to buy good health!

So many people are conscious that they are lacking direction in their lives. Perhaps they think that they have tried everything, but they have not found the security and joy that they long for. They feel like the Israelites in the days of Hosea. The strings of their bow are sagging and useless. They are weary from hurrying from place to place in the vain search for lasting happiness.

It is not sufficient to seek God merely for what we can get out of him. Some 'turn to the Lord' because they have found no satisfaction elsewhere, but do not truly repent. This is the folly of those who preach a 'You need Jesus' gospel. Although Joseph Hart rightly told the 'sinner, poor and needy,' that 'All the fitness he requireth is to feel your need of him', we need to make sure that we do not fall into the trap of giving the impression that deep, heartfelt repentance is an optional extra.

The only solution for sinners lies at Calvary. Those who are unconverted need to confess their sins and seek God's forgiveness. Believers who are spiritually jaded also need to return to God's training ground. He wants his people back in his squad. He longs for them to return to the discipline of daily prayer, study and regular fellowship with God's people.

12

The danger of complacency

Please read Hosea 8:1–8

During the 1930s life in Britain went on fairly smoothly. The economy was beginning to get back onto some kind of even keel after the depression of the former years and everyone was starting to feel more settled in an increasingly comfortable lifestyle. But there were a few politicians who irritated many people by their continual warnings about the growth of Nazi power. Large numbers of the population did not want to hear such words of gloom. They placed their faith in Mr Chamberlain, who had visited the German chancellor on a number of occasions. After the final visit the prime minister returned on 30 September 1938 and when he got off his plane at Heston Airport he held up a little piece of paper on which was Herr Hitler's signature. As it fluttered in the air he declared that it guaranteed 'Peace in our time'. A great sigh of relief went up throughout the land. Everyone was rejoicing—except those from Czechoslovakia!

However, amid all the euphoria of those days, every now and then, on very clear, cloudless days, the soft drone of an aeroplane engine could be heard as it flew high overhead. These were planes of the German air force, and all the while that people in Britain felt safe, these planes were busy taking photographs of England in preparation for a future invasion by the Nazis. In less than one year after Hitler's assurances that his aspiration for world conquest was at an end, he invaded Poland—and the terrible Second World War had begun.

In Hosea's days the feelings of the inhabitants of the northern kingdom of Israel were similar to those of the British people in the last years of the 1930s. It was not a high-flying spy-plane that flew over their land; it was 'an eagle', which was circling over them. And this powerful bird was patiently waiting for the time to pounce swiftly, suddenly and unerringly on them. The word used for 'eagle' in Hosea 8:1 can also be translated 'vulture'. Vultures only eat dead animals. In this passage the eagle, or vulture, represented the power of Assyria. The picture here, then, is one of impending judgement waiting to be unleashed upon the people of Israel.

In many ways the people of God today are like the Israelites in the days of Hosea. Christian believers are guilty of a number of bad habits; we shall see some of them outlined in this chapter.

The tendency of assuming that we are free from danger (8:1–3)
Israel placed great reliance on the fact that they were God's own, special people. That was, indeed, true; the Lord had rescued them from the slavery of Egypt. He had delivered them from the hands of their enemies on very many occasions. However, they had taken all these blessings for granted; they had fallen into a false sense of security. They felt that they needed do no more except to tell each other the ancient equivalent of 'Smile, God loves you!'

In thinking like this they were incredibly foolish. They had developed the bad habit of assuming that they could just sit back and do nothing, and God would protect them whatever happened. They were rather like those Christians today who know that salvation is of the Lord, yet think that nothing further is required of them in return for God's mercies.

The solemn fact was that Israel was in danger, very great danger. The eagle of Assyria was flying high over them. When it says in verse 1 that the 'eagle is over the house of the LORD', Hosea is not referring to the temple, but to the people of Israel. He speaks of 'my house' in the same way in 9:15. In Britain some firms still use this form of address. The very first job I had when I left school was with a commercial music library called 'The House of Goodwin and Tabb'.

Because Assyria was waiting to pounce upon them, God calls out, 'Put the trumpet to your lips!' This was a call to battle; it was an alarm. Just as in the Second World War sirens sounded when an air raid was imminent, so in those days a trumpet would be blown to give warning of the approach of an enemy (see also 5:8; Joel 2:1; Amos 3:6).

Why was the enemy waiting to descend upon them? It was not just because Assyria wanted to enlarge its borders. It was because the Lord was going to punish Israel for their sinful ways. Much earlier in their history, in the book of Deuteronomy, God had given the people warning of judgement upon them: 'The LORD will bring a nation against you from far away, from the ends of the earth, like an eagle swooping down, a nation whose language you will not understand, a fierce-looking nation without respect for the old or pity for the young' (Deuteronomy 28:49–50).

Although they may have known that God had said this,

they still did not feel that they were in danger. They probably thought, 'These things don't apply to us.' Whatever the case, the people did not take heed of the warning and, in failing to do so, they sinned greatly.

Hosea gives us some of the reasons why God was going to punish them. They had been very disobedient. God said that he would discipline them 'because the people have broken my covenant and rebelled against my law' (8:1). The Israelites, who thought that they were safe because they were God's precious possession, had foolishly failed to keep their side of the covenant which God had made with them.

A covenant is an agreement between two parties. In the case of Israel God promised to redeem his people from slavery and make them into a great nation. This covenant was ratified by the blood of the lamb shed on the first Passover night in Egypt (Exodus 12:13). That was God's part of the agreement. Israel's part was that they promised to keep God's law (Exodus 24:7).

When Hosea pointed out that they had not kept God's covenant they were highly indignant. They cried out to God (perhaps in sheer disbelief at what he was saying to them), 'O our God!' It seems that they were still prepared to admit that he was their God. That is why they said, 'We acknowledge you!' Despite their sinfulness they were not ashamed to acknowledge God. Yet he says, 'Israel has rejected what is good' (8:3). The reason God said this was because they had no real knowledge of their Lord. Hosea had told them in 4:6 that they had rejected knowledge and were going to be destroyed because of their lack of it.

They were like those people in the Gospels who called out to Jesus, 'Lord, Lord,' but Jesus had to tell them, 'I never knew you' (Matthew 7:23). The reason why he said that he never knew them was because they did not do what he told them to do (Luke 6:46). The life that God had set before the people of Israel was a good one but, by their disobedience to the covenant God had made with them, they demonstrated that they had rejected that good.

We now come to consider Israel's second bad habit. It is one which we recognize, because God's people today are inclined to indulge in this same attitude.

The habit of thinking that we know best (8:4–6)

God has given us intelligence, and we should use that to the best of our abilities. The Lord does not want us to be unthinking robots. Also as parents we desire to help our children grow up with the ability to manage their own affairs sensibly. We like to think that we are bringing them up to be able to look after themselves and make wise decisions in life. The Lord God Almighty treats us, his children, in the same way. He wants us to act shrewdly.

However, the people of Hosea's day had taken this principle far too far. They tried to take matters entirely out of God's hands. They set up their own kings and they chose their own princes (8:4). They did these things without taking into account God's revealed will. They failed to use the guidelines that he had given to them. They forgot that one of the first qualifications for leaders among God's people is that they should be godly.

In the same way when we think of choosing pastors, elders and deacons in the church, then we should take very careful notice of the guidelines laid down in 1 Timothy 3. These criteria must come before anyone's own personal preferences. That is why we should not just appoint people to office in the church because they are the most popular ones. God's concern is that

the leaders of his people should be men 'after his own heart' (see
1 Samuel 13:14).

Not only did the Israelites choose their own rulers; they
also chose their own way to worship. They made idols with
their own silver and gold. This was partly because it cost them
something! They gave, from their own possessions, that which
was precious and costly. But even though they may have thought
that they were still worshipping the one true God, they were
coming to him in a way which was an abomination to him.
They were conforming to the style of worship of the heathen
people around them. They had not learned the lesson of Aaron,
who made a golden calf in the desert (Exodus 32). They, too,
had broken the second commandment: 'You shall not make for
yourself an idol in the form of anything in heaven above or on
the earth beneath or in the waters below. You shall not bow
down to them or worship them' (Exodus 20:4–5).

This was just one more way in which the Israelites of Hosea's
time had broken the covenant. This was why God told them,
'Throw out your calf-idol, O Samaria!' He also declared that his
anger burned against them. His heart-cry was: 'How long will
they be incapable of purity?' (8:5).

We can hear God's bitter disappointment with his people,
which must have been rather like the agony of Hosea's heart
when he realized that he had been spurned by his wife in favour
of more exciting lovers.

Then the Lord pronounces his sentence upon the people:

This calf—a craftsman has made it;
    it is not God.
It will be broken in pieces,
    that calf of Samaria   (8:6).

Not only will the calf of Samaria be smashed; so also will the whole of the northern kingdom. This is because they made idols for themselves which were 'to their own destruction' (8:4).

The stupidity of worldly alliances (8:7–8)

We have seen in Hosea 7:11 how foolish the people were in turning to Assyria and to Egypt for help. Now the Lord outlines for them the consequences of this folly. He says that they are behaving like someone who is sowing in the wind.

Every spring when I open a packet of seeds to sow them in my garden, the wind starts to blow. The result is that a great many of the seeds do not land where I intend them to go. They end up in my neighbour's garden, or even further afield. So, when we think about a farmer sowing one of his fields with corn we can understand why God speaks of such a man being foolish if he does so on a windy day. The Lord says that this spells disaster. He will not get a decent crop from sowing in this way.

Paul spoke about this kind of thing when he wrote to the Galatians: 'The one who sows to please his sinful nature, from that nature will reap destruction' (Galatians 6:8). In going to Assyria for help (instead of turning to the Lord their God) the Israelites had sown for themselves wind—that is, vanity, illusion and nothingness. The preacher in Ecclesiastes wrote, 'I have seen all the things that are done under the sun; all of them are meaningless, a chasing after the wind' (Ecclesiastes 1:14).

The fruit that Israel was producing from its foreign alliances was like a stalk of wheat which had no head. It would 'produce no flour', and even if any grain was produced foreigners would gather it and reap the benefit of it (8:7).

Because Israel went up to Assyria for help (8:9) they were going to be 'swallowed up' (8:8). If they wanted to turn their backs upon God, who had saved them and loved them, then they would find that they would 'reap the whirlwind'. They would discover that their foreign alliances would not only prove fruitless (8:7), but would be downright destructive (8:8).

Because of their desire to be like the other nations, they would be swallowed up by them and end up as 'a worthless thing'! We, too, must beware of these dangers which will tempt us. We must beware of thinking that because we belong to the Lord then we are not in danger from the Evil One. Paul told the Corinthians, 'If you think you are standing firm, be careful that you don't fall!' (1 Corinthians 10:12).

Secondly, we must be careful lest we behave as though we can manage on our own without living according to the teaching of God's Word. The book of Proverbs tells us, 'Trust in the LORD with all your heart and lean not on your own understanding' (Proverbs 3:5). Finally, we must remain free from the entanglements of worldly involvement. John tells us, 'Do not love the world or anything in the world. If anyone loves the world, the love of the Father is not in him' (1 John 2:15). May the Lord not have to say of us, 'How long will they be incapable of purity?' (see 8:5).

13

God's answer to disobedience

Please read Hosea 8:9–14

Those of us who regularly drive on the roads sometimes wonder whether we have gone straight through a light that was at 'red'. One morning I had been going along a road near my home which has traffic lights that only work at peak times. After I had passed these I found myself wondering whether the lights had been 'red' and I had failed to stop. When this possibility crossed my mind my first thought was: 'If the lights were against me and I did not stop, did anyone see me, and if so will I be prosecuted?'

When we break any law it is instinctive for us to try to avoid being caught. The people of the northern kingdom of Israel had broken many of God's laws, yet they appeared to have no conscience about it; they did not see why they had done any wrong.

When we examined the first part of Hosea 8 we considered how foolish it is to think that we are safe, or that we know best.

Here, in the second half of the chapter, we shall take note of what God has to say about the behaviour of his people.

The danger of wandering (8:9–11)

God had been telling Ephraim, or the northern kingdom, that their nation was going to be swallowed up by those whom they had regarded as their protectors (8:8). They assumed that it was a sensible thing to turn to the mighty power of Assyria. We saw in 7:11 how they had *turned* to Assyria for help; now, when we come to 8:9, we notice that they had not only turned to Assyria, they had actually 'gone up to Assyria'. In other words, they had ignored the Lord their God, and treated him as though he were unable to help them. Instead they had turned towards a foreign power, a nation who did not acknowledge the one true and living God. God's people went to a nation that worshipped heathen gods, and these gods were just as abominable to the Lord as the Baals of the Canaanites.

Therefore, from turning towards Assyria, the Israelites had thrown in their lot with the Assyrians and had marched northwards. When people look in the wrong direction, they automatically turn their backs upon the right one. So, Ephraim's sin was not just in going up to Assyria, it was in turning their backs upon the Lord their God.

Much earlier in biblical history, when the land had to be divided between the herdsmen of Abraham and those of Lot, we read that, when he was given the choice of which direction to go, Lot chose the fertile plain of the Jordan. We are specifically told that *near* this area was the city of Sodom and that 'The men of Sodom were wicked and were sinning greatly against the Lord' (Genesis 13:13). The Authorized Version tells us that Lot 'pitched his tent toward Sodom' (Genesis 13:12). Then, only a few verses later, we discover that Lot was soon actually living *right in Sodom* itself (Genesis 14:12). We, too, if we keep looking towards those things which are unhelpful, will quickly find ourselves living among, and becoming involved with, the evil of the world around us.

When Ephraim went among the nations (8:8) the nation corrupted herself. She thought that she would get great benefit from doing this. Little did she realize that she would soon be 'swallowed up' and become a 'worthless thing' in God's sight (see 8:8).

Hosea now changes the figure as he tells us that Ephraim is 'like a wild donkey wandering alone' (8:9). Donkeys were usually domestic animals, and they were generally kept in groups so that they could be useful to their masters. Yet God says that Ephraim had rebelled against this and had become 'wild'. In doing so the Ephraimites had wandered away from the rest of God's people and had turned to their own way. In other words, they had chosen to please themselves.

Later on in the history of God's people Jeremiah was also going to compare them to donkeys. In Jeremiah 2:23–25 he says:

> How can you say, 'I am not defiled;
> I have not run after the Baals'?
> See how you behaved in the valley;
> consider what you have done.
> You are a swift she-camel
> running here and there,
> a wild donkey accustomed to the desert,
> sniffing the wind in her craving—
> in her heat who can restrain her?
> Any males that pursue her need not tire themselves;
> at mating time they will find her   (Jeremiah 2:23–24).

In this passage God is comparing the behaviour of his people to that of wild animals out in the desert. The female animals, when they are on heat, allow their scent to waft in the breeze in the hope that any passing male will come to them.

The Lord uses this well-known behaviour to say to his people, 'In your craving after alliances with Assyria you are behaving the same way as you did when you turned to worship the Baals.' This is the same kind of unfaithfulness that Gomer showed towards her husband, Hosea, when she chased after other men—flaunting herself to gain their admiration and their money! God says of them, 'You are no better than wild donkeys wandering alone. You are selling yourself to any lover who will take you.' Then he gives them this advice:

> Do not run until your feet are bare
>   and your throat is dry.
> But you said, 'It's no use!
>   I love foreign gods,
>   and I must go after them'   (Jeremiah 2:25).

A little later he continues:
> Look up to the barren heights and see.
>   Is there any place where you have not been ravished?
> By the roadside you sat waiting for lovers,
>   sat like a nomad in the desert.
> You have defiled the land
>   with your prostitution and wickedness.
> Therefore the showers have been withheld,
>   and no spring rains have fallen.
> Yet you have the brazen look of a prostitute;
>   you refuse to blush with shame   (Jeremiah 3:2–3).

In this passage Hosea gives Ephraim a similar warning of God's judgement. He says, 'Although they have sold themselves among the nations, I will now gather them together.' God was going to gather them together, not in a joyful family reunion, but in order to bring judgement upon them for their waywardness in turning from him. The Bible speaks of judgement in similar terms in Joel 3:2 and Zephaniah 3:8. God's gathering of them will result in their utter destruction: 'They will begin to waste away under the oppression of the mighty king' (8:10).

The insincerity of some religious observance (8:10-13)

The Israelites had made a great show of their religion. They had built many altars for sin offerings. At first sight, we might have thought this was a good sign. It looked as if they were recognizing that they needed to confess their sin to God. However, the Lord said about these actions, 'Though Ephraim built many altars for sin offerings, these have become altars for sinning.'

Sin offerings were prescribed in Leviticus 4:1-5:13 for the washing away of sins which had been committed in ignorance. Then, after the ceremony, the priests ate the meat of the animals which had been sacrificed. However, in the time of Hosea it seems that many people participated in the feast after the sacrifices had been offered. We can see, then, that they not only regarded it as a light thing that they had sinned; they offered sacrifices with the attitude that Paul speaks about in Romans 6:1: 'Shall we go on sinning, so that grace may increase?' To this the apostle says a very definite 'No'. But these people of Ephraim would not have agreed with Paul. They would have said, 'Let's keep sinning so that we can have great numbers of feasts after the sacrifices.'

God said of these people, 'They offer sacrifices given to me and they eat the meat, but the LORD is not pleased with them.' Next he tells them what will happen to them because he is not pleased with them: 'He will remember their wickedness and punish their sins,' and 'They will return to Egypt' (8:13).

The name 'Egypt' spelled slavery to the Israelites, as we saw in looking at Hosea 7:16. This is the reason why he speaks of judgement: 'They offer sacrifices given to me and they eat the meat.' It was the feasting that they were interested in, rather than the confessing of their sinfulness. Lloyd Ogilvie says, 'The love of eating flesh superseded the love for the Lord.' He concludes, 'When our worship is not in keeping with what God desires from us, it degenerates into a worship of ourselves.'

Ephraim not only twisted the meaning of sacrifice, but also treated God's law with disdain. The Israelites were certainly aware of what the Lord had written in his law. They would have known, too, that this law was written with the finger of God upon two tablets of stone when he was up on Mount Sinai with Moses (Exodus 31:18). They would have been aware that it had been engraved right into the stone and that it could not be erased. They would have been taught from childhood the meaning of God's laws, and their obligation to obey them. Yet, even when the people were in danger, they ignored God's laws. God's indictment of them was that 'They regarded [these laws] as something alien.' In other words, they said, 'These laws are nothing to do with us'.

How much this is like the attitude of many people today to the commands of God! They treat his laws as merely something which might *possibly* give them a little guidance if it suited them at the time. The Israelites condemned in this passage were rather like the person who wrote to Anne Atkins, the 'agony aunt' of the *Daily Telegraph* newspaper, saying that the God who wrote the Ten Commandments was not the kind of God for her. Mrs Atkins replied that, whether we like it or not, God is God and he cannot be moulded into the image we desire. So many people flout God's laws in these days. Before we raise our hands in horror at the suggestion that we, as Christian people, ignore just laws, let us ask ourselves questions like, 'Do I realize that I am breaking the Tenth Commandment when I covet another person's expensive car, or lavish foreign holiday?'

Likewise there are many people who claim to be Christians, yet they blatantly disregard God's laws and see no need to repent of their behaviour. The writer to the Hebrews says of such people, 'How much more severely do you think a man deserves to be punished who has trampled the Son of God under foot, who has treated as an unholy thing the blood of the covenant that sanctified him, and who has insulted the Spirit of grace?' (Hebrews 10:29).

The response of God (8:14)

The Lord's answer to the activities of Ephraim is summed up in the five words that we find at the beginning of verse 14: 'Israel has forgotten his Maker.' God's people had experienced the Lord's deliverance from the bondage of Egypt. They had known the Lord's blessings on many occasions since that time, but in the time of Hosea they had forgotten their God. It was even more serious than that: they had rejected all knowledge of the Lord (see 4:6). Instead of remembering the Lord and waiting patiently for him to save them, they had been frantically occupied in a building programme. They had built many altars, but had put them to wrong use (8:11). They had built palaces, and Judah, too, had 'fortified many towns'. Because this activity was all directed towards wrong ends, God was going to do something. He was going to send the fire of judgement upon their cities, and he was going to 'consume their fortresses'.

This passage teaches us the folly of man, and the response of God to man's foolish works. Hosea 8 tells us about some of the energy the Israelites had exerted. In verse 9 they wandered alone. In verse 11 they built many altars. In verse 12 they had regarded God's many laws as alien. Finally, in verse 13 they offered sacrifices and took pleasure in eating the delicious meat with its appetizing aroma.

We now see what God says he will do in response to their actions. In verse 10 he says that they will 'waste away' and suffer under the 'oppression of the mighty king'. In verse 13 we see that he is 'not pleased with them ... he will remember their wickedness and punish their sins'. In verse 14 we read that they had forgotten their Maker and that he 'will send fire' to consume their fortresses and destroy their cities. What a sad indictment upon God's people! They had been chosen to be his own blood-bought possession, yet they had turned away from him and had turned towards other powers. Therefore, he was going to judge them and destroy them (8:4).

This God of the Israelites is still the same God who controls the universe today. His laws and his demands have not altered. He requires each one of us to obey him and not to regard his law as alien to us. The terrible thing is that, if we continue sinning against him to the end of our days, then he will destroy us, as he destroyed the northern kingdom. We shall be punished in the fire of his judgement. The Lord Jesus Christ spoke a great deal about the fires of hell. He condemned those whom he described in the parable as 'goats'—that is, those who did not honour him or his people. He says to them, 'Depart from me, you who are cursed, into the eternal fire prepared for the devil and his angels' (Matthew 25:41).

However, because of God's gracious love, there is still hope for those who have been wandering far off from God. They have only to confess their sin to the Lord Jesus Christ, who bore in his body on the cross the sins of those who will turn to him in repentance and faith. He calls such to turn away from the path which leads to hell, and turn to him, the only one who is able to save.

14

Who wants to listen to bad news?

Please read Hosea 9:1–9

There are some people who seem to take great delight in bad news. Everything they tell you is either about someone who has died in dreadful circumstances, or about some awful tragedy which has occurred. They never seem to be able to look on the bright side of things. I knew an old lady once who enjoyed going to funerals! She was rather like one of the characters in Tommy Handley's wartime radio show, *ITMA*, whose catchphrase was: 'It's being so cheerful as keeps me going.' And the character's name? Mona Lott! We probably all know people who are inclined to be like that. However, although there are a few people around who seem to enjoy being miserable, by and large most of us like to concentrate on the joyful things of life.

Certainly as Hosea 9 opens, the people of Israel were feeling like that. Why should they not enjoy themselves? They had been blessed with an excellent harvest and, following all the hard work of gathering it in, we see them in this passage joyfully celebrating 'harvest home'. Well, at least, they were having a great time until Hosea arrived on the scene.

Joy taken away (9:1–4)

Harvesting is very hard work. The wheat can only be gathered in while the weather is fine. This means that everyone is called in to help when the corn is ready to be reaped and gathered in. Harvesting days last a long time, are very hard work and the breaks for food and drink are very short and infrequent.

Even when the grain has been stored away that isn't the end of the matter. It is also essential to store it safely, and guard it well. If this is not done then robbers will creep in and steal it. Throughout history there have always been those who have been content to let others do all the hard work, and then benefit from the efforts of their labour.

It was for reasons of this kind that it was the custom for the workmen to remain on guard in the barns after the harvest had been brought in. The farm-workers would probably be far too exhausted to return home anyway until they had rested a while. In any case, they would want to stay to enjoy the great thanksgiving festival that would follow.

At the end of the harvest, while the men were relaxing in the barns, it was not uncommon for women of easy virtue to go and join them, and offer the use of their bodies for money. A number of the men would avail themselves of this 'pleasure'. Perhaps some of the workers saw it as a reasonable reward for all their hard work. Others—younger men, for instance—would be caught up in the general excitement. They, too, would succumb to the lure of the prostitutes.

That was the scene at a typical harvest celebration—as the feasting began. The Israelites thought they were thanking God for the blessings of the harvest but, in reality, they were really praising Baal for his bounty, because it was to these heathen gods that they had offered sacrifices in the hope of a good harvest.

Hosea used these well-known details to point out that these farmers were just like the whole of the northern kingdom. They assumed that an abundant harvest was a sign of God's blessing upon them. There are many in our day who think along the same lines. Merely because a person's business prospers, that does not necessarily mean that God is rewarding him! On the other hand, just because a person is poor in this world's goods, that does not automatically mean that he is under the curse of God.

The Bible says some very harsh things about rich people, and this should make us realize that riches are not inevitably a sign of God's approval. For example, Jesus said, 'It is easier for a camel to go through the eye of a needle than for a rich man to enter the kingdom of God' (Matthew 19:24). Thomas Brooks put it like this: 'You may as well fill a bag with wisdom, a chest with riches, or a circle with a triangle, as the heart of man with anything here below. A man may have enough of the world to sink him, but he can never have enough to satisfy him.' And Matthew Henry commented, 'Man takes great pains to heap up riches, and they are like heaps of manure in the furrows of the field, good for nothing unless they be spread.'

The Bible also has much to say about those who are poor in this world's goods. The Lord helped many people who were poor. On one occasion he told those who were holding a banquet to invite the poor, the crippled, the lame and the blind (Luke 14:13). Often we see that God has a very special concern for those who are poor and needy (e.g. see Psalm 40:17). However, the balance is well struck in Proverbs 30:8: 'Give me neither poverty nor riches, but give me only my daily bread.'

The New Testament contains a very helpful illustration of a rich man who had a bountiful harvest (Luke 12:13–21). He had so much corn that he did not know where to put it all. It does not seem to have occurred to him that he could give some of it away to others. Certainly there is no indication that he expressed thanks to God. The Lord himself tells us that he was 'not rich towards God' (Luke 12:21). The only thing that this wealthy farmer was concerned about was where to put all his harvest. Therefore, he enlarged his barns to make room for it. Then he sat back with great satisfaction and told himself, 'You have plenty of good things laid up for many years. Take it easy; eat, drink and be merry.' But God had other ideas. He said, 'You fool! This very night your life will be demanded from you. Then who will get what you have prepared for yourself?'

In much the same way as God addresses the rich fool (as this man is usually called), Hosea strides into the excitement of harvest thanksgiving with these blistering words: 'Do not rejoice, O Israel; do not be jubilant like the other nations' (9:1). Why does he say that? He gives the reason: 'For you have been unfaithful to your God.' Once again this word 'unfaithful' comes to the fore. God had been faithful to his promise to them, but his people had turned their backs upon him and his Word. Then, for the last time in his prophecy, Hosea uses the figure of the prostitute. He said, 'You have been unfaithful to your God; you love the wages of a prostitute at every threshing-floor.'

He once again accuses them of the guilt of spiritual adultery. They much preferred to show their love to Baal, rather than to the one who loved them and saved them by the blood of the Lamb. But this time they were not going to be left unpunished. We can almost hear God's majestic voice ringing round the whole of Israel as Hosea speaks the words of the Lord: 'They will not remain in the LORD's land' (9:3).

Think what an awful shock that must have given them to have heard those words. God does not even address them directly. He does not say, '*You* will not remain in *my* land.' They have to hear it at second hand as Hosea passes on God's words to them. They had abused the privileges of living in the promised land. They needed to be reminded that it was not their land. It was God's land. Because of their disobedience they were going to be removed from it.

They had been warned of what would happen to them if they were unfaithful to their God: 'Be careful that you do not forget the LORD, who brought you out of Egypt, out of the land of slavery. Fear the LORD your God, serve him only and take your oaths in his name. Do not follow other gods, the gods of the peoples around you; for the LORD your God, who is among you, is a jealous God and his anger will burn against you, and he will destroy you from the face of the land' (Deuteronomy 6:12–15). God had also told them that if they did not obey the Lord their God and carefully follow all his commands and decrees, then they would be scattered among the nations: 'The LORD will scatter you among all nations, from one end of the earth to the other. There you will worship other gods—gods of wood and stone, which neither you nor your fathers have known. Among those nations you will find no repose, no resting place for the sole of your foot. There the LORD will give you an anxious mind, eyes weary with longing, and a despairing heart. You will live in constant suspense, filled with dread both night and day, never sure of your life. In the morning you will say, "If only it were evening!" and in the evening, "If only it were morning!"— because of the terror that will fill your hearts and the sights that your eyes will see. The LORD will send you back in ships to Egypt on a journey I said you should never make again. There you will offer yourselves for sale to your enemies as male and female slaves, but no one will buy you' (Deuteronomy 28:64–68).

What does Hosea mean when he tells the people that they are going to 'return to Egypt and eat unclean food in Assyria'? Egypt and Assyria are situated in exactly the opposite directions in relation to Israel. The clue to his meaning is found in the word 'return', which, of course, means 'go back'. This is what they had been doing in recent days. They had been turning their backs on God and going back to heathen worship. Therefore, they were going to go back—not literally to Egypt, but to what Egypt symbolized, that is, slavery! They were going to be in bondage to the Assyrians. In captivity they would not be able to eat the kosher food of Israel. Lloyd Ogilvie comments: 'They had worshipped false gods in their own land; now they would be forced to eat food that was taboo. They would have to stomach their own apostasy!' In Assyria they would not be able to offer sacrifices to please God. Neither would they be able to 'come into the temple of the LORD'. They would be far off from the temple at Jerusalem. They would also be cut off from the land of God (see comments on 8:1).

Precious possessions mutilated (9:5-6)
Hosea then challenges them to consider their future. The philosophy that says, 'Let us eat and drink, for tomorrow we die' (quoted by Paul in 1 Corinthians 15:32), does not take into account the future. The Israelites had this large harvest, but what good would it do them when Assyria swooped down on them and took them away captive?

Hosea told them that if they escaped with their lives, 'Egypt [would] gather them and Memphis [would] bury them.' The Israelites would have known what he meant, even if it is a little puzzling for us. First, we note that he again mentions

Egypt. Egypt, as we have seen, was the place of slavery, and in Egypt there was a very famous city called Memphis, which was particularly noted for its huge gravesites or pyramids, built for its pharaohs during the Fourth Dynasty (c. 2700–2200 BC). That was about 2,000 years before Hosea's time. In other words, then, death was all they could hope for, and under the cruel hands of the Assyrians they would long for it to come so that they could be set free from the excruciating pain of their cruel torture.

Next comes a hint of what will become of their riches. The world says, 'You can't take it with you.' These people would have to leave behind many of 'their treasures of silver' (9:6). These were going to be overrun by thorns and briars, as were all their dwelling-places. Like the rich fool, they would have to leave all their riches behind them. In the same way as God said to him, 'Who will get what you have prepared for yourself?' he says here to the Israelites, 'Corruption will come upon the things that you hold dear.'

God's prophets ignored (9:7–9)
Although dreadful judgement was about to descend on Israel, they did not seem to be aware that this was going to happen. This is why God instructs Hosea to say to them, 'The days of punishment are coming, the days of reckoning are at hand. Let Israel know this' (9:7). Israel had means of hearing the voice of God. He had set among them prophets who declared his Word. However, these prophets were ignored. They were regarded as fools and maniacs, and all because they did not say what the people wanted to hear.

However, it was not the prophets who were fools; it was the people. They never stopped to consider whether the men to whom they listened were godly or righteous. They only wanted to hear pleasant things from them. God told them through the prophet Micah, 'If a liar and deceiver comes and says, "I will prophesy for you plenty of wine and beer," he would be just the prophet for this people!' (Micah 2:11).

We can see, then, that although the people of Israel were in great danger, they did not want to listen to those who could see into God's future plans. The prophets, along with God, were the watchmen over Ephraim (9:8). Watchmen were set up on high vantage-points so that they could see far into the distance and sound a warning if an enemy was approaching. God's prophets were watchmen; they could see danger on the horizon. Habakkuk, for instance, said:

> I will stand at my watch
>   and station myself on the ramparts;
> I will look to see what [God] will say to me,
>   and what answer I am to give to this complaint
>
> (Habakkuk 2:1).

Although God had appointed these men, the people did not listen to them. Snares were awaiting these prophets wherever they went and they faced hostility even in God's house.

This section ends with a dreadful denunciation of the people of God. The Lord said, 'They have sunk deep into corruption' (9:9). To illustrate how serious the Lord considered their behaviour to be, he told them that they were behaving like those of Gibeah, a reference to the events recorded in Judges 19:16–30. The people of Israel would have known about one of the most scandalous incidents in the Bible, when some wicked men of Gibeah committed a heinous crime. Having been denied homosexual sex with a man who was a guest in their town, they then gang-raped a concubine until she was dead. God's own people in Hosea's time had been behaving in similarly appalling ways. Therefore God was going to 'remember their wickedness and punish them for their sins' (9:9; cf. 8:13). They would be deported, never to return to the land of God.

How dreadful is the judgement of God on those who are unrepentant! What a contrast this is to those words recorded in Jeremiah 31:34 where he speaks of the new covenant which is going to be established through the death and resurrection of the Lord Jesus Christ. At that time it will be said:

> 'No longer will a man teach his neighbour,
> > or a man his brother, saying, "Know the LORD,"
> because they will all know me,
> > from the least of them to the greatest,'
> > declares the LORD.
> 'For I will forgive their wickedness
> > and will remember their sins no more'   (Jeremiah 31:34).

15

God's warning of fruitlessness

Please read Hosea 9:10–17

One year I planted a golden hop, *Humulus Lupulus* 'Aureus'. I put it against one side of my wooden rose arch, right next to *Rosa* 'Great Maiden's Blush'. But this was a mistake because the pale pink of the Alba rose gets lost among the large golden leaves of the hop. As my hop emerged from the ground that first spring I carefully trained its tentacles around and up the arch—but you should see it now! It is so huge that it has almost completely engulfed the rose arch. I have even had to hack some of it down because it is so rampant.

That is how God intended Israel to be. I want my golden hop to be prolific, just as God desired that Israel should be a vine which would spread throughout the land and produce an increasingly large amount of fruit year after year (see Hosea 10:1). One place where we can read about this is the incident when the patriarch Jacob gathered all his children together to bless them before he departed from this earth. He described

Joseph as 'a fruitful vine, a fruitful vine near a spring, whose branches climb over a wall' (Genesis 49:22). That was a picture of what all Israel should have been. But sadly, as Hosea passes on to them God's message, we see that the reality was very different.

God looks backwards in time (9:10–13)
In Hosea 9:1, and again in verse 5, God spoke directly to the people, but here in verses 10–13 and 15–16 the Lord addresses Hosea and tells him about Israel (or Ephraim). There are painful things which have to be said. However, God's righteous anger is such that it will not even let him speak to the people. They have been disobedient once too often.

Again we can see the love which wells up in the heart of God, their Father. This is demonstrated very many times in this prophecy. Hosea shares that longing for Israel to return to their God in a wholehearted manner, just as he yearns for his wife to return to him and set up a loving, godly family once again.

The Lord reminds the people of the delight that he experienced in the early days of the history of the Israelite nation, when he made his covenant with them in the desert (see, e.g., Exodus 24:7). He expresses this by painting a picture of surprising contrasts. What do we expect to find in a desert? We anticipate that there will be sand—and not much else. We certainly do not think of finding luscious, juicy grapes in the dry, hot, harsh desert. But that is exactly what God found in Israel. Of course, he knew they were there, but the Lord talks in terms of 'finding them', using language that we can understand. He often uses figures like this. He speaks about guiding people with his eye, and saving them with his powerful, outstretched arm— even though God is Spirit, and spirits do not posses human body parts!

We understand, therefore, from this passage that, just as any weary traveller through the desert would count it a surprising blessing to come upon an oasis filled with vines covered in grapes, so God took much pleasure in his people, who promised to obey him, and in return he covenanted to care for them.

To ram the message home, the Lord said that, in the past, Israel had also been like the early fruit on the fig tree. Personally, I never liked figs until some years ago when our family was on holiday in northern Greece. We were walking back to our apartment, after a very hot day on the beach, when a lady told us that we could pick and eat the figs off a tree growing by the side of the track. When we did so we discovered that they were delicious, apart from the sticky sap which stuck our fingers together!

So God says that when he found Israel in the desert, 'It was like seeing the early fruit on the fig tree' (9:10). This early fruit is a delight, not just because it is the first of the fruit, but also because it is the best. Isaiah had expressed similar thoughts:

That fading flower, his glorious beauty,
    set on the head of a fertile valley,
will be like a fig ripe before harvest—
    as soon as someone sees it and takes it in his hand,
    he swallows it

(Isaiah 28:4).

Hosea uses another similar figure in 9:13, conjuring up a picture of fertility, when he says, 'I have seen Ephraim, like [prosperous] Tyre, planted in a pleasant place.' Similarly, the righteous man in Psalm 1 is compared to a tree planted (by God) beside streams of water.

Just as we see the huge difference between luscious grapes and the barren desert, an even greater, and more terrible contrast, burdens the heart of God. The Lord starts with that worrying word, 'But'.

I remember the first time I read Dr Martyn Lloyd-Jones' sermon on Ephesians 2:4. Using the previous verses, he had painted an awful picture of the hopeless condition of men and women living without Christ, 'fulfilling the desires of the flesh and of the mind', living as 'children of disobedience' and 'children of wrath'. At this point the preacher had thundered out those two tremendous words, *'But God,'* before going on to expound the text which continues, 'But God, who is rich in mercy, for his great love wherewith he loved us, even when we were dead in sins, hath quickened us together with Christ' (Ephesians 2:2–5, AV).

However, when we come to look at Hosea 9:10, it is not with any sense of rapture that we read the word 'but'. Here we are reminded of the way the word is used when speaking of Naaman. The biblical account begins by telling us that he was 'captain of the host of the king of Syria', and that he 'was a great man with his master, and honourable, because by him the LORD had given deliverance unto Syria: he was also a mighty man in valour'. Then, however, we read these devastating words: *'but* he was a leper' (2 Kings 5:1, AV).

Israel had started out so well but, before very long, the people had began to drift away from their promise to follow only the Lord. When they came to Baal Peor (a mountain to the eastern side of the Dead Sea, in the region of Moab) we read of their wicked behaviour: 'While Israel was staying in Shittim, the men began to indulge in sexual immorality with Moabite women, who invited them to the sacrifices to their gods. The people ate and bowed down before these gods. So Israel joined in worshipping the Baal of Peor' (Numbers 25:1–3).

Here in Hosea we observe that they were doing just the same kind of thing. They were guilty of immorality, of turning their backs upon the Lord and serving false fertility gods (the Baals) instead of the true God. Do you detect the anguish in God's voice? He had done so much for them, but now they had forgotten him.

Jeremiah tells the same kind of story:

The word of the LORD came to me:
'Go and proclaim in the hearing of Jerusalem:
"I remember the devotion of your youth,
    how as a bride you loved me
and followed me through the desert,
    through a land not sown.
Israel was holy to the LORD,
    the first-fruits of his harvest;
all who devoured her were held guilty,
    and disaster overtook them,"'
    declares the LORD.
Hear the word of the LORD, O house of Jacob,
    all you clans of the house of Israel.
This is what the LORD says:
'What fault did your fathers find in me,
    that they strayed so far from me?
They followed worthless idols
    and became worthless themselves.
They did not ask, "Where is the LORD,
    who brought us up out of Egypt
and led us through the barren wilderness,
    through a land of deserts and rifts,
a land of drought and darkness,
    a land where no one travels and no one lives?'
                                    (Jeremiah 2:1–6).

The Lord Jesus Christ has the same message for the church at Ephesus: 'You have forsaken your first love' (Revelation 2:4). The bride left standing at the altar, jilted by her lover, presents a very sad picture, and one that evokes much sympathy. The picture painted by Hosea is one of God waiting for the affection of his people, while they have given it to another.

Jeremiah picks up this same theme. God said:

> I brought you into a fertile land
> to eat its fruit and rich produce.
> But you came and defiled my land
> and made my inheritance detestable   (Jeremiah 2:7).

We see the result of their spiritual adultery in Hosea 9:11-13. 'Ephraim's glory will fly away like a bird' (cf. the earlier statement that 'An eagle is over the house of the LORD', 8:1). They had been a glorious people in the past, but now they had rejected their God and his love, they were about to discover that their glory had swiftly flown away, just like a bird.

Their situation would be like that of Israel in the days when the ark had been captured by the Philistines. After hearing the news, the wife of Eli's son Phinehas gave birth to a child, and with her dying breath, 'She named the boy Ichabod, saying, "The glory has departed from Israel"—because of the capture of the ark of God and the deaths of her father-in-law and her husband. She said, "The glory has departed from Israel, for the ark of God has been captured"' (1 Samuel 4:21-22).

In Hosea's day the glory had departed from Ephraim because of their continual disobedience to God's Word. In 9:3 God had said that their land would be taken away from them. In verse 6 they were told that they would lose all their wealth. And now, in verse 11, God says that there will be 'no birth, no pregnancy, no conception'. Then he adds, 'Even if they bring up children, I will bereave them of every one' (9:12). No progeny meant no future. Therefore, this part of the nation would be utterly destroyed. This was solely because they had failed to keep God's law.

Hosea's prayer (9:14)

As God was grieved, so Hosea's heart was broken, too—first by the lost of his own wife's affection, and then by the apostasy of God's people. We see, and we share, his confusion.

Any pastor joins with Hosea in grieving. One of the saddest things a pastor has to do is to watch while those who started out so well fall away from Christ. Hosea prays to God. His opening words recall the prayer of the psalmist:

> Ascribe [or 'give', AV] to the LORD, O mighty ones,
>   ascribe to the LORD glory and strength.
> Ascribe to the LORD the glory due to his name;
>   worship the Lord in the splendour of his holiness
>
> (Psalm 29:1).

The prophet, however, scarcely knows what to pray—just as we, too, are so often at a loss to know what to ask God for when we are praying for those who are behaving in a wayward manner. Therefore, Hosea prays, 'Give them, O Lord—what will you give them?' He cannot bear to pray for their slaughter, so he prays that they will be barren: 'Give them wombs that miscarry and breasts that are dry.'

This prayer that God's people would be fruitless is an awful request to make. We are reminded of the passage in Isaiah 5, where the Lord compared Israel to a vineyard and asked, 'What more could have been done for my vineyard than I have done for it?' Yet when it came to harvest-time, what did he find? He said, 'When I looked for good grapes, why did it yield only bad?' (Isaiah 5:4).

God looks backwards and forwards (9:15–16)

He takes the people back in their imagination to Gilgal. This place had featured prominently in Israel's past history. There the people had crossed the River Jordan as they finally entered the promised land (Joshua 4:19–24). It was also at this place that Saul was confirmed as the first King of Israel (1 Samuel 11:15). But that king rebelled against God's Word and was rejected by the Lord because he had 'turned away' from God and had not carried out his instructions (1 Samuel 15:10).

Now the people had once again turned away from God and had turned to the Canaanite Baals. These Baals were fertility gods, and the Israelites worshipped them because they hoped for increased fruitfulness from the land. God says to them, 'Because of all their wickedness in Gilgal, I hated them there.' That word 'hated' is very strong. Nor does he stop there. He continues, 'Because of their sinful deeds, I will drive them out of my house'—that is, out of the land (as in 8:1).

God's hatred is very severe. He will wreak vengeance on the ungodly. He hates sin and all those who engage in sinful ways. That is why he says, 'I will no longer love them; all their leaders are rebellious' (like King Saul). Once more he returns to an agricultural theme, comparing the nation to a mighty tree, when he says,

> Ephraim is blighted.
> > their root is withered,
> > they yield no fruit.
> Even if they bear children,
> > I will slay their cherished offspring.

For an Israelite this was a dreadful thing to hear. Blessing was always expressed in terms of children. In Psalm 128:3–6 we read:

Your wife will be like a fruitful vine
    within your house;
your sons will be like olive shoots
    round your table.

Again we find the agricultural theme of fruitfulness. The psalmist continues:

Thus is the man blessed
    who fears the LORD.
May the LORD bless you from Zion
    all the days of your life;
may you see the prosperity of Jerusalem.
How is that prosperity measured?
May you live to see your children's children.
Peace be upon Israel.

It was sheer folly for Israel to turn away from the one and only true God and turn instead towards false gods. Once God had loved his people, but now, as had been prophesied in the naming of Hosea's daughter 'Lo-Ruhamah', he would 'no longer show love to the house of Israel' (1:6).

The result of the people's dabbling in Canaanite religion was that they would be punished by being deported from their land, losing their possessions and being denied offspring. David Hubbard comments: 'Canaanites were driven out so that Israel could enjoy God's gift of the land; now Israel were to be driven out because of their assimilation to Canaanite practices.'

Hosea's response (9:17)

Hosea cannot but agree with God—the one he calls 'my God'. Ephraim will be rejected because they had rejected God and had not obeyed him, his law or his Word. He says, 'They will be wanderers among the nations.' In other words, like Cain (Genesis 4:14), they will have no settled home in the world. They are blighted. 'Their root is withered' and they will 'yield no fruit' (9:16).

How dreadful is God's vengeance upon those who disobey him! They will be unfruitful and will eventually wither away. All that will be left will be a dry, dead stump of a once-flourishing tree. But what does Isaiah say about this stump? 'A shoot will come up from the stump of Jesse; from his roots a Branch will bear fruit' (Isaiah 11:1). That shoot is none other than the Lord Jesus Christ. He is that 'tender shoot' who was to spring up 'like a root out of dry ground' (Isaiah 53:2). God had pronounced severe judgement on sinners. That punishment is nothing less than death. And who among us can honestly say that we do not deserve to be punished for our sin?

The good news of the gospel is that Christ has borne that punishment in our place, if we are 'in him'—in other words, if we have put our trust in him. Isaiah says,

> It was the LORD's will to crush him and cause him to suffer,
>   and though the LORD makes his life a guilt offering,
> he will see his offspring and prolong his days,
>   and the will of the LORD will prosper in his hand
>
> (Isaiah 53:10).

What a marvellous promise! Although the disobedient people of Israel in Hosea's day would have no children, through Christ's atoning death on the cross many will be 'born of God' (John 1:13).

16

Divided loyalties

Please read Hosea 10:1–8

I must confess that when I was a boy the 'Saturday Morning Cinema Show' held a great fascination for me. One of the main highlights of that programme was the 'cowboy film'. This involved the cowboys in a great deal of fast horse-riding, while chasing villains. After very many twists and turns, just before the end-titles, the good guys always caught the bad guys and then handed them over to the law. In those black-and-white films it was easy to tell the 'goodies' from the 'baddies' because the 'goodies' wore white hats and the 'baddies' had black ones. It never seemed to occur to the 'baddies' to cheat by wearing white hats; I suppose in those days even the crooks knew the rules!

The other thing I remember was those scenes where the magnificent Red Indian chief stood outside his tepee, towering over the cowboy. He would stand there, with his arms folded and his flamboyant feathered head-dress hanging down his back. Quite often there would be a scene where the white man would approach the chief and start to discuss some scheme or other with him. While the chief was considering the proposition he would suddenly pause, frown and then say, in a harsh tone, 'White man speak with forked tongue.' In other words, because of his previous experience of the white man, the Indian chief felt that he couldn't trust his word. He 'spoke with forked tongue', saying one thing, but meaning another.

The Bible has a great deal to say about people who use language like that, either with the purpose of deliberately deceiving someone, or of vacillating from one opinion to another. Twice James speaks about such people. He tells us about a double-minded man and comments that he is unstable in all he does (James 1:8); he also writes about those who are sinners, and he addresses them as 'you double-minded' (4:8). In the book of Psalms we have the same thought: 'I hate double-minded men, but I love your law' (Psalm 119:113).

So, as we look at the first ten verses of Hosea 10, we shall see that God continues to denounce the people of the northern kingdom and says that they cannot be trusted because 'Their heart is deceitful.' As we examine this passage we shall see several ways in which God's people were guilty of divided loyalties.

Israel was guilty of selfishness (10:1–2)

As in 9:10, this passage starts off with God recalling that 'Israel was a spreading vine.' Not only that, but 'He brought forth fruit', and 'His fruit increased' (10:1). In other words, Israel was just like a vine with luxuriant growth, that was full of fruit.

That is exactly what a farmer wants from a vine, or any of his produce. His requirement is that it should produce an abundance of fruit and at the same time that this should be of excellent quality. Such a crop would have brought great joy to the heart of the farmer! There would have been plenty of grapes for eating, wine-making and also for selling on to others—to make a good profit.

A vine like that would have brought a great deal of benefit to its owner; yet we see a different picture when we learn how Israel's spreading vine fared. Hosea tells us that 'Israel was a spreading vine' which 'brought forth fruit for himself'. What does he mean by saying the fruit was 'for himself'? By 'himself' he obviously does not mean God. He means the people of Israel.

This is the scene. There is a vine which produces a sumptuous crop, but instead of the grapes bringing blessing to the farmer who owns it, and who has cared for it over the years, the vine produces a crop for its *own* glory!

Jeremiah speaks of the same phenomenon when he compares God to a potter. The Lord says, 'O house of Israel, can I not do with you as this potter does?' He continues: 'Like clay in the hand of the potter, so are you in my hand, O house of Israel' (Jeremiah 18:6).

Israel had forgotten that their purpose was to bring glory and honour to their God. Instead they thought they existed for their own benefit. Hosea pointed out that this was the result of false thinking. He said, 'As his fruit increased, he [Israel] built more altars.' In fact, the land became scattered with altars. 'As his land prospered, he adored his sacred stones.' The prophet means that instead of returning praise and honour to God for all his blessings to them, the people of Israel directed their energies towards the worship of false Baals. They built altars to these fertility gods and they decorated these altars with ever more costly precious stones. But they must have known that God did not wish to them act like that.

Jesus also spoke about his people as being a fruitful vine. He emphasized that they could only produce good fruit as they continued to abide in him. He said, 'Remain in me, and I will remain in you. No branch can bear fruit by itself; it must remain in the vine. Neither can you bear fruit unless you remain in me' (John 15:4).

Therefore, the conclusion that the Lord arrives at concerning Israel is that 'Their heart is deceitful' (10:2). They had divided loyalties because, on the one hand, they gave the impression that they were worshipping Yahweh, when all the while their desires were directed towards pleasing the fertility gods, or Baals.

When we looked at Hosea 8:2 we saw that they were calling out to God, but their cry was only half-hearted. They only called out to the Lord because they knew that it was their duty to do so. Even though they pretended to be worshipping God, they were actually owning allegiance to the Baals. We can see, then, why God called them double-minded. It was because their hearts were filled with deceit.

Whatever we might say with our mouths, it is in our hearts that our emotions are firmly seated. We must make sure that we are sincere in our worship of God.

Because the people of Israel were deceitful, God pronounced that they must bear the consequences of their guilt. In the meantime God was going to remove their objects of false religion. He was going to demolish—utterly smash—their altars. He would see that their sacred stones were destroyed.

Israel was guilty of making false promises (10:3–4)
The people had forgotten that God was their King (1 Samuel 12:12). They had been given human kings to rule them, but many of these had proved to be ungodly. Therefore, their king would soon be taken from them, when Assyria invaded the whole of their northern kingdom.

When we come to verse 3 they appear to be acknowledging that they knew why their king was going to be taken from them. It was because they 'did not revere the LORD'. Sadly, as they say this, there seems to be not the slightest glimmer of repentance in their hearts. Even if there was, their hearts were so deceitful that no one would know if their sorrow was genuine. They compounded their lack of repentance by saying, 'Even if we had a king, what could he do for us?'

Like so many people today, they appear to have lost all sense of the power of God to rule over them and keep them safe. One commentator says, 'They forget their own history in which God has acted powerfully, and they begin to look to other entities as the source of strength and the hope for deliverance.'

Many kings of the northern kingdom had been particularly corrupt and deceitful. They had entered into various kinds of agreements in which their word had proved to be unreliable. An example of this is recorded in 2 Kings 17. Hoshea, Israel's last king, had entered into covenant with the king of Assyria. But some time later he broke his oaths to Assyria and turned to Egypt instead (2 Kings 17:3,4). This piece of 'covenant-breaking' was to bring to an end the existence of the nation of Israel.

The breaking of solemn promises was an evil which was endemic among people of all classes. We have already seen how badly the priests and other leaders behaved, and this attitude affected the entire nation. In Hosea 4:9 we read, 'It will be: Like people, like priests.' God went on to say, 'I will punish both of them for their ways and repay them for their deeds.'

Their 'false oaths' and breaking of agreements led to lawsuits springing up like 'poisonous weeds in a ploughed field'. Noxious weeds might grow in the hedgerows, but not in land which has been well cultivated and prepared for producing good food! They were like the crop which an enemy sowed while the farmer slept (see Matthew 13:25). 'False oaths' and unjust behaviour had sprouted where there should have been justice and righteousness. Amos, too, makes a similar plea: 'Let justice roll on like a river, righteousness like a never-failing stream!' (Amos 5:24).

The matters addressed in these verses are very pertinent to the people of God today. We should not only be people of the book, but should also be men and women of our word. We ought to be open and honest in all our dealings with everyone, believer and non-Christian alike. And we should not be double-tongued, nor make promises which we have no intention of keeping.

Israel was guilty of false worship (10:5–6)
We have often come across this 'calf-idol of Beth Aven' (which means 'house of wickedness' and was formerly called Bethel— 'house of God'). What was Israel doing in Beth Aven? The people were crying over their calf-idol. They were mourning because it was to be taken away into Assyria.

The 'great king' (that is, the King of Assyria) wanted it because it was gold-plated and therefore valuable. In Hosea 2:8 we learn that, just as this calf had been covered in gold, so Israel had lavished silver and gold on Baal. The calf had been set up in the first place by Jeroboam I to make it unnecessary for his people to cross the border to visit the temple at Jerusalem in order to worship.

Jerusalem was in the southern kingdom of Judah. In 1 Kings 12:29 we read about the erection of calves both at Bethel, which was in the southern extremity of the northern kingdom, and also at Dan, which was right up in the north. The people had gladly gone to worship the Lord at these places—as they thought. Except that it was not to Yahweh that they were giving allegiance; it was a wooden idol that they were worshipping. The golden calf looked good, gleaming in the sunlight, but Hosea said it was merely a 'wooden idol' (see 10:6).

Israel had quickly forgotten Moses' anger (and God's) when their forefathers had worshipped the golden calf in the desert (Exodus 32). Evangelicals—and others—find it difficult to understand how some people can kneel down in front of a statue of Mary, or some other saint, and repeat a form of words as though were praying to God. If such people are relying on the statue to listen to their prayers they need to be told that they are merely bowing down to an object made of wood or stone.

We, too, must not think that we are offering true worship to God if we are really worshipping 'a golden calf'—that is, if we are worshipping anything which is less than God himself. For example, if we take great pride in being part of a growing church, which is ever more adventurous, then we are in danger of giving reverence to 'a golden calf' instead of the Lord. If we are spending our time and energy in amassing wealth, prestige and public acclaim, instead of obeying the Lord and his Word, then we are guilty of worshipping a golden calf called 'Success'.

The result of all this so-called worship of the golden calf at Beth Aven was that Ephraim was going to be disgraced, and Israel would be ashamed. In Hosea 8:5–6 God had told the people to throw out their calf-idol, but they had ignored him and still worshipped it.

What did their precious golden calf do for them when Assyria finally swooped down on the whole of the northern kingdom? It just stood there glistening in the sunshine, displaying its beauty, in much the same way as the gleaming golden roof of the Dome of the Rock dominates Temple Mount in the city of Jerusalem today, in all its magnificent splendour.

The calf, upon which the people had placed so much reliance, 'stood mute and helpless as the Assyrians systematically dismantled Israel. Israel's glory had become her shame.' All those who pin their hopes on false gods will find that they receive no word, no answer to their aspirations. The only hope that anyone can have is through trusting in the one true and living God, who can only be approached through the shed blood of the Lord Jesus Christ. All other ground will prove to be 'sinking sand'.

Israel would come under divine judgement (10:7-8)

Israel discovered, as will everyone else, that on the Day of Judgement all human religion will prove to be of no avail. The fact that these people worshipped at the high places (4:13) did them no good. If they had pleaded with God and told him that they were sincerely trying to please him, it would have proved useless. Their enemies would still have destroyed them. They would have discovered that, however sincere they were in their religion, they were sincerely wrong! Everything upon which they placed their hopes—the glory of Samaria and the power of its king—was going to be swept away.

They would find that they had no more power to save themselves, or their people, than a small twig has when it is caught up in a powerful, fast-flowing flood of water. Their altars, upon which they offered many costly sacrifices and which they adorned with costly stones (10:1), would be abandoned. They would be so neglected that weeds would grow up over them. 'Thorns and thistles will grow up and cover their altars' (10:8). God was going to turn these precious places of worship into 'a thicket', and wild animals would roam all over them (2:12). The people were about to discover that all their own efforts to please

God were going to be demolished under the fierce hand of the Assyrians.

Worse still, it was not merely that God would stand back and allow this to happen to the people—but, because of their sin, he would actually instigate it. In the previous chapter he had said, 'I hated them' and 'I will drive them out of my house' (9:15).

Because of this judgement, they would call upon the mountains to fall on them and crush them. They would try to escape the punishment of God by being killed in a great rock-fall.

How had the hills that surround Israel formerly been looked upon? The psalmists had said many things about them, for example:

> I lift up my eyes to the hills—
>   where does my help come from?
> My help comes from the LORD,
>   the Maker of heaven and earth   (Psalm 121:1).

In another psalm we read:

> As the mountains surround Jerusalem,
> so the LORD surrounds his people
>   both now and for evermore   (Psalm 125:2).

Yet another psalm says:

> Your righteousness is like the mighty mountains,
>   your justice like the great deep.
> O LORD, you preserve both man and beast   (Psalm 36:6).

But now these hills, which had protected them for generations, were being called upon to destroy them. Jesus spoke about the coming destruction of Jerusalem, which happened in AD 70: 'They will say to the mountains, "Fall on us!" and to the hills "Cover us!"' (Luke 23:30). Also John, in the book of Revelation, describes the great day of God's judgement which is yet to come upon the whole world: 'Then the kings of the earth, the princes, the generals, the rich, the mighty, and every slave and every free man hid in caves and among the rocks of the mountains. They called to the mountains and the rocks, "Fall on us and hide us from the face of him who sits on the throne and from the wrath of the Lamb!"' (Revelation 6:15–16).

Great judgement was going to fall upon Israel—so great that they would call on the mountains to cover them from it. This final judgement on the world has still not come. One day every one of us will have to stand before the judgement seat of Christ (2 Corinthians 5:10). There will be no escape for anyone.

People in our day need to heed the warning of these verses. It will not save them to seek comfort in saying, 'I often went to church and sat through many long sermons.' Whatever good anyone has done in this world, it will never alter the fact that we are all sinners in God's sight. The only hope for any of us is to hide ourselves in Jesus Christ.

17

It is time to seek the Lord

Please read Hosea 10:9–15

Many people still remember hearing Richard Dimbleby's heart-rending broadcast from Belsen Concentration Camp, following its liberation in 1945. He described the experience as 'the most horrible day of my life'. The vast majority of people living in Britain during the war years had no idea that such inhuman atrocities were being meted out on huge numbers of poor, helpless men and women—just because they were Jewish, or gypsies, or they belonged to some other minority which did not meet with Hitler's approval. As, in the calm of their homes, they listened to that historic broadcast, they were struck dumb with the horror of it all.

Enormous repugnance fell upon the listeners as the BBC reporter described a poor demented mother, screaming at a soldier for milk for her baby. She trust the tiny mite into his arms and then ran away. Richard Dimbleby described the scene as the soldier carefully opened the bundle of cloth and uncovered the emaciated body of a baby who had been dead for days!

Even over half a century later, those who were among the liberators on that day must shudder every time they hear the name of Hitler, or that of Belsen. Even those of us who merely heard the broadcast still recoil at the mention of them.

A similar, and equally horrifying, disgust would invariably have caused icy shivers to run down the spines of the people of Israel when Hosea reminded them of what Shalman had done at the devastation of Beth Arbel. History tells us nothing about this man, Shalman, or the town where his evil deeds took place. But the people of Israel evidently knew what happened there— and they no doubt shuddered at the very mention of these two names.

The things which evil men do to pregnant women on the field of battle are too horrifying for us to describe here, but we can read about some of the loathsome acts which were perpetrated in 2 Kings 8:12-13 and Amos 1:13. Other scriptures tells us about equally terrible atrocities which were inflicted on helpless citizens (see Psalm 137:8-9; Isaiah 13:16; Nahum 3:10).

So we come to look again at the state of the northern kingdom of Israel.

Israel was still sinful (10:9-10)

A terrible sin had been committed at Gibeah many centuries before Hosea's time. When we looked at Hosea 9:9 we referred back in Israel's history to this event, which we find recorded in Judges chapters 19-21. As a result of that horrendous crime perpetrated at Gibeah, the rest of the tribes of Israel rounded on Benjamin, the tribe to which the town of Gibeah belonged. These other tribes inflicted great slaughter on Benjamin. The battle was so fierce that only 600 men were left alive from the tribe of Benjamin. Because of their sinful deeds at that time, terrible disaster befell the tribe, and every Israelite would have known about it and its consequences!

What had the Israelites learned from those things? Absolutely nothing. We can say that because we find them still behaving in the same sinful fashion. It was for this reason that Hosea tells them, 'Since the days of Gibeah, you have sinned ... and there you have remained' (10:9).

The prophet goes on to remind the people of the consequences of Gibeah's sin: 'Did not war overtake the evildoers in Gibeah?' He means that, as the rest of the tribes of Israel had punished the tribe of Benjamin very severely in the days of the judges, so God himself was going to punish Israel in a similar way in Hosea's days. However, on this occasion it was not the rest of the tribes who were going to inflict the punishment; it would be the heathen nations who would gather against them—notably the dreaded Assyrians. They would 'put' the Israelites 'in bonds'. And, God tells them, this will be 'for their double sin'.

What does he mean by this? Firstly, as we have seen, they sinned at Gibeah, and then, secondly, they remained in their sin. In that sense their sin was double. Jeremiah (who prophesied to the southern kingdom) puts the double sin of God's people in a very picturesque way. The southern kingdom sinned just as badly as the northern kingdom. Speaking through Jeremiah, God told Judah,

> My people have committed two sins [AV 'evils']:
> They have forsaken me,
>   the spring of living water,
> and have dug their own cisterns,
>   broken cisterns that cannot hold water   (Jeremiah 2:13).

In other words, the people of Judah had turned their backs upon the true God (who was the only one who could satisfy their thirst for living water), and had turned aside to their own ways (i.e. they followed the Baals)—thinking they would find satisfaction in that quarter. In doing so they had discovered that the quest for salvation through their own efforts alone brought them no lasting peace or security!

No doubt the people asked the prophet when this punishment was going to be inflicted upon them. He told them that their God said it would be 'when I please'. Man can try by his own efforts to obtain his salvation. He can perform his good works, he can engage in his private religious devotions and he can attend all the church ceremonials that he likes, but it is what pleases God that counts, and it is when God pleases that blessing (or judgement) will come upon the people.

Paul tells us that there is a day coming (when God pleases) on which every knee will bow to the Lord and every tongue will confess that Jesus Christ is Lord. Some will do so willingly, because they have loved and served Jesus during their lifetime, but others will be forced to bow the knee to him, because they have turned their backs on the Lord throughout the whole of their lives (Philippians 2:9-11). There is a time coming in the future—only God knows when—at which Christ will appear in judgement upon all mankind. Paul tells us that 'We will all stand before God's judgement seat' and, on that day, 'Each of us will give an account of himself to God' (Romans 14:10,12). When will this happen? How long have we got before we need to repent of our sins? We do not know. But it will happen 'when God pleases', and there will be no escaping it. Therefore, we need to make sure that we are ready.

Israel had been chosen for blessing (10:11-12)
Israel is described here as 'a trained heifer'. She is pictured as a

domestic animal, a useful beast. God had trained her and she had gladly served him. While she did so, she was able to reap the reward of a faithful servant. Deuteronomy 25:4 tells us, 'Do not muzzle an ox while it is treading out the grain.' This was so that the oxen could eat some of the corn while they were walking upon it to thresh it. This was an easy and pleasant task for the animals to perform. That is why God said that Ephraim 'loves to thresh'. The Israelites had been trained by God to serve him— and to delight in his service!

Throughout their lives God had continued to show them his grace. Hosea, speaking the words God had given him, continues to use agricultural metaphors. He tells the people, 'Sow for yourselves righteousness.' If they did so then they were promised that they would eventually 'reap the fruit of [his] unfailing love'.

They would have known that farming is a long process. First, the land has to be broken up by being ploughed. Then the seed has to be sown in the fertile ground. That is man's part in the harvest process, but it also needs God to work before a harvest can be reaped. The fields not only need sunshine, they also require rain to fall upon them. Paul, speaking about the spiritual harvest of precious souls, said, 'I planted the seed, Apollos watered it, but God made it grow' (1 Corinthians 3:6). So God tells Israel, 'Before you can receive blessing you will have to obey my law.' This is what he means by saying that he will 'put a yoke on her fair neck'. He is talking about his law, his Word. At first sight it might seem that this yoke of keeping God's law would be a great trial for the people. They would feel restricted by being tied up but, in fact, they were secure. Jesus said, 'Take my yoke upon you and learn from me, for I am gentle and humble in heart, and you will find rest for your souls.' Then he adds, 'For my yoke is easy and my burden is light' (Matthew 11:29-30). For us to take God's yoke upon us means that we should ask him to make us humble and teachable, desiring only to live to please him.

In verse 11 God speaks of Ephraim, Judah and Jacob. Here, 'Ephraim' means the northern kingdom, sometimes called Israel. 'Judah' is the southern kingdom, and 'Jacob' means both of the kingdoms, before they were split. Jacob was the name first given to the man who was afterwards named Israel (see Genesis 32:28).

In order to get this rich harvest, God tells the people that they must 'break up your unploughed ground' (10:12). In a literal sense they knew that the land had to be ploughed before it was suitable to sow seed into it. God now told them that their hearts needed to receive the seed of the Word of God. That seed would not take root within them and produce fruit unless the conditions were right.

Their hearts and their thoughts were, at that time, very hard indeed. They had been steeped in sinful ways. They had turned their backs upon the one true and living God. And they had turned aside to false gods. Therefore, they needed to break up the hard ground of their hearts. In other words, they required to be softened, and made willing and ready to receive and obey God's Word. It was high time for them to do this. They had left things far too long. They needed to prepare themselves to receive the Word of the Lord.

In order to bring them to their senses, Hosea issues this clarion call: 'It is time to seek the LORD.' Many people fall into the trap of thinking that there is plenty of time to get right with God. But time is a very precious commodity that is fast running out. None of us knows how much longer we have left to live upon this earth. Any ninety-year-old will verify how quickly the time goes. In the words of Isaiah, we all need to 'seek the LORD while he may be found; call on him while he is near'. Isaiah continues:

Let the wicked forsake his way
    and the evil man his thoughts.
Let him turn to the LORD, and he will have mercy on him,
    and to our God, for he will freely pardon   (Isaiah 55:6-7).

When the Israelites were in the desert God also told his people that if they were to 'seek the LORD your God, you will find him if you look for him with all your heart and with all your soul' (Deuteronomy 4:29). Is that what Israel did? No. Hosea tells us that instead of breaking up their unploughed ground and showing righteousness, they had 'planted wickedness'.

Israel will suffer for their disobedience (10:13-15)

Hosea now explains what the Israelites had done. They planted wickedness, instead of righteousness (10:13). They knew what they ought to do, but they did the opposite.

One day when I was playing badminton, I saw where my opponent was planning to return my serve, so I rushed to the place in time to intercept the shuttlecock. I then went and hit it into the net. My partner said, 'Bad luck! You knew what you should have done.' And I muttered, 'It's like life. We so often know what we ought to do, but we don't do it.'

Following the agricultural order of things, because they had sown wickedness, they automatically reaped evil. However, instead of feasting on good fruit, they ate the fruit of deception. They were deceived themselves, and they led others astray too.

Anyone who follows the devil's direction, and indulges in sinful disobedience to God, will reap the devil's harvest. Jesus tells us that '[The devil] was a murderer from the beginning, not holding to the truth, for there is no truth in him. When he lies, he speaks his native language, for he is a liar and the father of lies' (John 8:44).

Why will Israel reap these things? It will be because they have 'depended on [their] own strength'. They were too proud to ask for help from God. 'I will do it my own self,' is what little children often say. And they end up in a mess as a result of their independent spirit. So it is with the person who goes through life thinking that he can manage without God. He is a fool. The psalmist tells us, 'The fool says in his heart, "There is no God"' (Psalm 14:1). Also the person who says, 'O yes, I believe that there is a God up there somewhere,' but who takes no notice of what God says, is an even greater fool.

The other reason why the people of Israel were going to reap destruction was the fact that they depended on 'many warriors'. They had made foreign alliances, and they put their trust in these. However, they discovered that, at the time when they most needed support, their allies were to be found wanting. Our motto ought to be that of the psalmist, who said, 'Some trust in chariots and some in horses, but we trust in the name of the LORD our God' (Psalm 20:7).

The consequence of all this was that Israel found that she was defeated. 'The roar of battle' rose against them, and all their fortresses, by which they had set such store, were devastated.

Hosea went on to say that all this would come to pass 'when that day dawns'. Dawn is so often the symbol of a better hope. We speak of the dawning of a new day. But for the people of Bethel (the king's sanctuary) it was going to mean complete destruction.

It will be the same for all those who fail to turn to the Lord, and prefer to go their own way (which is always the way that leads to destruction). Proverbs 14:12 tells us, 'There is a way that seems right to a man, but in the end it leads to death.'

There is only one way for a nation, or an individual, to find

God, and that is by coming in humble repentance to the one who called himself 'the way and the truth and the life' (John 14:6).

18

The loving heart of God

Please read Hosea 11:1–11

One Sunday morning when my eldest son was about two years old he was dressed up in a lovely blue silk suit ready for church. We left him in the lounge, knowing that he was safe there. However, when we went to collect him, we discovered that he had been exploring the contents of the coal scuttle. He had passed the time by taking very large lumps of coal, holding them tightly against his brand-new silk suit, and then disposing of them in each of the armchairs and on the settee!

I suppose most people remember a great deal about the early life of their first-born child. I certainly recall the excitement when Tim took his first, faltering steps with the aid of a baby-walker. I remember walking alongside him, holding out my hands to make sure that I caught him if he was in any danger of falling. Later on, when he grew a little bolder, he charged along with his 'walker' and often tripped and hurt himself on the path, but I would be there to 'kiss it all better'.

In this remarkable passage in Hosea chapter 11, we have an amazing glimpse of the compassionate heart of God as he cares for his children. Calvin was worried about any suggestion that God has feelings, because he is unchangeable. This is why he wrote in his commentary on Hosea at this point, 'God is exempt from every passion.' However, Erroll Hulse maintains that the Reformer said this because he did not wish anyone to think of the Lord as one who changes his mind because of pressures outside of himself. To use Erroll Hulse's words, '[God] cannot be pushed around.' Although that is true, Hosea 11 teaches us that God does have deep feelings of love. We human beings have emotions and we are made in the image of God. Even more importantly, in the life of God's Son, the Lord Jesus Christ, we find one who lived a 'life full of rich emotion'.

The wayward son (11:1–7)

We have seen Israel described in many different ways in the book of Hosea. In 9:10 the nation is compared to a fig tree, and in 10:1 to a spreading vine bringing forth an increasing amount of fruit. But here in chapter 11 God describes Israel in more human terms. In his use of such language we see the tenderness of God displayed in a deeply compassionate way (as we find it nowhere else in Scripture).

God calls Israel 'my son'. Speaking like the Father he is, he reminds his children of the time when they (as a nation) were new-born while they were in the bondage of Egypt. God had instructed Moses to tell Pharaoh, 'Israel is my first-born son' (Exodus 4:22). While they were in Egypt God loved them. He provided for them a deliverer (Moses) and he fed them along the way (see Exodus 16:4). While they were still in Egypt, God heard their cry for deliverance and saved them. He brought them out of Egypt and, eventually, into the promised land, where he enabled them to drive out their enemies and to enjoy the fruit of this 'land flowing with milk and honey'.

How did Israel show their gratitude to God, their Father, who had done so much for them? They were surprisingly ungrateful. As we have seen in every chapter in the book of Hosea so far, 'They sacrificed to the Baals and they burned incense to images' (11:2). In their captivity in Egypt they had remained separate from the heathen Egyptian gods. However, when they reached the promised land they foolishly adopted the ways of the Canaanites.

They did not appear to realize that their loving Father God was caring for them. They did not seem to understand that it was he who healed them every time they fell and hurt themselves. Apparently they forgot (or took for granted) the fact that he had led them through the desert and, indeed, throughout the rest of their lives—and that he had done so 'with cords of human kindness'. He loved his children deeply, and he showed his love in many ways.

Like a kind farmer, he carefully 'lifted the yoke' of restrictions (which was beginning to chafe them) 'from their neck and bent down to feed them' (11:4). There are various interpretations of this verse, but whether the figure is still that of a loving father, or that of a kind farmer, the message is very clear. God showed his loving-kindness to them. He even 'bent down' to feed them. In the same way God, in Christ Jesus, came down to this poor, sin-sick earth and fed his people with heavenly manna (see John 6).

God showed his love to Israel by teaching them and protecting them throughout their early years. He told his people, through Isaiah, about his watchful care over them:

He tends his flock like a shepherd:
    he gathers the lambs in his arms
and carries them close to his heart;
    he gently leads those that have young   (Isaiah 40:11).

In Psalm 121 we read:

He who watches over you will not slumber;
indeed, he who watches over Israel
    will neither slumber nor sleep.
The Lord watches over you—
    the Lord is your shade at your right hand;
the sun will not harm you by day,
    nor the moon by night.
The Lord will keep you from all harm—
    he will watch over your life;
the Lord will watch over your coming and going
    both now and for evermore   (Psalm 121:3–8).

So, like a kind, loving human father, God 'taught Ephraim to walk, taking them by the arms'. The Lord taught them to walk in his ways. He taught them to obey his laws. The commandments are not like a heavy yoke, which bites into an ox's neck. They are given for the benefit and blessing of all those who obey them. God actually took delight in Israel.

The Lord your God is with you,
    he is mighty to save.
He will take great delight in you,
    he will quiet you with his love,
    he will rejoice over you with singing   (Zephaniah 3:17).

Yet the more God called Israel, the further they went away from him. He warned them that 'Even if they call to the Most High,' just as he said they should in 7:14, 'he will by no means exalt them' (11:7). However, instead of returning to God, they turned away from him. The consequences were going to be very painful for them (as Hosea had told them many times in the previous chapters). They would return to the kind of bondage their forefathers had experienced while they were in Egypt. They would have the Assyrians ruling over them. Homer Hailey says, 'The Assyrian will be their king because they had refused to have Jehovah as King.' And all this danger awaits them for one reason only. God explains: 'My people are determined to turn from me.' We can almost hear the anguish of God's heart as he cries, 'My people [the ones I have done so much for] are determined to turn from me'—the only one who can help, heal, cleanse and save them.

Matthew quotes verse 1 in connection with the Lord Jesus having been taken as a young child into Egypt (Matthew 2:15). This was to escape the wrath of King Herod, who destroyed all the babies under two years of age who were born in Bethlehem. The evangelist tells us that, in the same way that Israel was called out of Egypt to the promised land, to be a light to the nations, so the Lord Jesus Christ was brought out of Egypt in order to grow up into manhood and to be a light to the Gentiles.

The resolve of the Father (11:8–9)
When we reflect on all that Hosea had to suffer in being married to his continually unfaithful wife, we can imagine the turmoil that must have been tormenting his heart and mind. He was at a loss to know what he should do with her. Would it be sensible to take her back again, only to see her carrying on in her infidelity? That would certainly give him more heartache in the future. Surely she had gone too far in her adultery for any reasonable person to forgive her! The real question for the prophet was: 'Could he love her again?' Yet, remarkably, that was exactly what God called him to do: 'The LORD said to me, "Go, show your

love to your wife again, though she is loved by another and is an adulteress"' (Hosea 3:1).

However, this book is not really about Hosea and the state of his heart and mind; it is about God. Nowhere else in the Bible are we permitted to look into the anguish of God's heart as we are in Hosea 11:8. Campbell Morgan, twice minister of Westminster Chapel in London, illustrated God's love for his own by telling a story about the terrible polluted London fogs of the 1920s and 1930s. One day he was standing in a bus queue behind a mother and child. Suddenly a bus pulled up. When their turn came to board the bus the mother stepped on board and the bus then drew away and disappeared into the gloom— leaving the child on the pavement. The child, of course, began to cry and was extremely frightened because his mother had gone. Campbell Morgan then poses the question: 'Who was most in torment over this loss—the child or the mother?' We have no problem in saying, 'The mother'. So why do some say that God does not have feelings? Surely, they have misunderstood the love of God as he grieves over the spiritual adultery of his children.

This is what we see in verse 8. God loves his children deeply, yet because of their iniquity, his concern for justice had pronounced judgement upon them, and fearful destruction. We noticed this just a few verses earlier where he lashed out at them: 'Swords will flash in their cities, will destroy the bars of their gates and put an end to their plans' (11:6). But it is at this point that we perceive that our God is not unfeeling. Despite the reasonableness of their punishment his heart cried out:

> How can I give you up, Ephraim?
>> How can I hand you over, Israel?
> How can I treat you like Admah?
>> How can I make you like Zeboiim?   (11:8).

This is a reference back in Israel's history to the time when the cities of Admah and Zeboiim had been destroyed in God's fierce anger along with sinful Sodom and Gomorrah (see Genesis 10:19; 19:24–29). Yet the Lord continues: 'My heart is changed within me; all my compassion is aroused' (11:8). Therefore, he concludes: 'I will not carry out my fierce anger, nor will I turn and devastate Ephraim.'

But how can he change his mind when he has threatened such judgement upon these sinful people? God is not fickle, as men are. He does not say one thing and mean another. He answers this by explaining: 'I am God, and not man—the Holy One among you.' He means that, because of his nature, he has decided that, after all, he 'will not come in wrath'. He calls himself the Holy One who is among them. Verses 10 and 12 are the only places in Hosea where God refers to his holiness. So what does all this mean when he says that he will not carry out his fierce anger? We know that God cannot lie (Hebrews 6:18). So why did he say that he would destroy them (e.g. in 8:4), but now say that he will not come in wrath?

History tells us that the northern kingdom was captured and taken away into Assyria. As a nation, they never returned. However, when we read 1 Chronicles 9:1–3 we see that there were a number of the Israelites who moved south to Judah before the Assyrians attacked Ephraim. We are given a list of these people, who were later taken from Jerusalem into captivity in Babylon. Among these were some from the tribes of Benjamin, Ephraim and Manasseh who lived in Jerusalem at the time of the Assyrian attack on the northern territory.

So, we can see, then, that verses 8–9 are not talking about God changing his mind, as men change theirs. Quite evidently this message of hope was given to those citizens who had left Israel.

It was they, and their descendants, who were faithful to God's covenant.

In these verses we see something of the compassionate heart of God towards those of his people who repented and turned again to him. In Isaiah 57:17 we read God saying, 'I was enraged by his sinful greed; I punished him, and hid my face in anger, yet he kept on in his wilful ways.' But he follows this, in verse 18, with: 'I have seen his ways, but I will heal him; I will guide him and restore comfort to him.'

God never changes. He will punish sin with judgement—the judgement of everlasting suffering in hell—but he will freely forgive all those who do change and who turn to him in repentance and faith. That is the message that Jesus came to give, and that is the blessed salvation which he went all the way to the cross to bring about.

However, if we today act like the bulk of the northern kingdom of Israel, who persisted in their waywardness, then we shall perish in our sin. Hosea's message holds good for all of us. All these many centuries later, it is still true that 'It is time to seek the Lord' (10:12). The Holy One is still among us and he calls us to follow him, just as Jesus called his disciples to follow him (Matthew 4:19).

The welcome homecoming (11:10-11)
For those who were faithful to God and his Word there would be a sure homecoming. They would not remain in exile for ever. Hosea prophesied that 'They will follow the Lord,' and he would lead them. The Lord was going to call out with an unmistakable cry: 'He will roar like a lion.' He would be the one who triumphs, as was Jesus Christ, the lion of the tribe of Judah (Revelation 5:5). When God, the lion roars, 'His children will come trembling' (not with fear, but with excitement) 'from the west.' They will

come with alacrity, 'like birds from Egypt' (i.e. out of bondage). And they will come 'like doves from Assyria'. They will no longer be the silly doves of 7:11, but they will come with swiftness and joy. Furthermore, God is going to 'settle them in their homes'. This is so certain that the Lord 'declares' it to be so. They are no longer merely passing through the land. They will be settled—permanently—in their homes. They will no longer live in an alien land (as we do at this time). As the old Negro spiritual puts it, 'This world is not my home; I'm just a-passing through.'

Peter tells us about this home at the end of this world. He says, 'The day of the Lord will come like a thief. The heavens will disappear with a roar; the elements will be destroyed by fire, and the earth and everything in it will be laid bare.' This ought to frighten us if we do not belong to the Lord. Peter therefore concludes: 'Since everything will be destroyed in this way, what kind of people ought you to be? You ought to live holy and godly lives as you look forward to the day of God and speed its coming. That day will bring about the destruction of the heavens by fire, and the elements will melt in the heat. But in keeping with his promise we are looking forward to a new heaven and a new earth.' He tells us that this is 'the home of righteousness' (2 Peter 3:10-13).

19

Return to your God!

Please read Hosea 11:12-12:14

When I was a boy I was sent to Sunday School each week. Occasionally we had 'object lessons'. For these we had to take along something which illustrated a Bible story. Shortly after we had had a lesson on 'Jacob's ladder', I tried to paint a picture depicting this to take along as my object, but my efforts were not very successful. My father, whose artistic abilities I have not inherited, saw what I had done and decided to paint the picture for me. So, on the following Sunday, I proudly submitted this painting for the competition. I was thrilled when it was announced that I had won a prize for it (I think it was second prize). On the way home I distinctly remember one of my friends whispering to me, 'I'm going to tell Mr Hudson that your dad did that painting.' (Mr Hudson was our Sunday School Superintendent.) I do not know whether he ever did report me, but now I want to confess my deception, even though it is well over fifty years late! I expect Mr Hudson has been in heaven for many years, but it was wrong of me—and

I have never forgotten the deception I carried out that Sunday afternoon. However, ever since that time I have had a rather soft spot for Jacob, because Jacob changed his ways and he found God at Bethel (see 12:4).

Encouragement from the past (11:12–12:6)
After so much doom and gloom during the earlier part the book, we ended our previous chapter on a high note. In the latter part of chapter 11 of his prophecy, Hosea told us about repenting souls flying back to God. The Lord promised to settle them in their homes and assured them that they would dwell securely there for ever.

As we launch into the section beginning at Hosea 11:12, we find we are back on the old familiar judgemental tack. In our first verse three names are mentioned: Ephraim and Israel (both names for the northern kingdom), and Judah (the southern kingdom). We see that they are all spoken of as ganging up against the Lord:

> Ephraim has surrounded me with lies,
> > the house of Israel with deceit.
> And Judah is unruly against God,
> > even against the faithful Holy One   (11:12).

Hosea here paints a picture similar to that of a city which is being besieged by an invading army. Only here it is God who is under siege and the army which is opposing him is his own people!

This is the charge that God brings against them: the northern kingdom is surrounding the Lord with lies and deceit, and the southern kingdom is behaving in an unruly manner. So far Hosea's prophecy has been directed mainly against the northern kingdom, but now we see that the sin of the southern kingdom is also being taken into account. (Some Bible versions translate this verse in a way which draws a contrast between the behaviour of Judah and that of the northern kingdom. For example, the NKJV says, 'But Judah still walks with God' and the AV, 'Judah yet ruleth with God.' However, the NIV rendering is in line with the charge which the Lord has to bring against Judah in 12:2. Kidner tells us that '"Judah is still known by God" ... is based on the Septuagint.')

In 12:1 God describes the activity of Ephraim (the northern kingdom). The people of Ephraim were behaving selfishly; they were concerned solely about the welfare of their own nation. This verse is to do with food, protection and trade. These are certainly three things that any government ought to be concerned about. However, a righteous government would want to provide *good* food, *wise* protection and *healthy* trade. But this was not what Ephraim was doing. They were 'feeding', not on something which would sustain them, but 'on the wind'. To be more precise, they were pursuing the east wind—and doing so 'all day', every day.

Hosea also uses this figure of the wind in 8:7 and in 13:15. The 'east wind' is the one which blows across the baking-hot sands of Arabia, scorching everything before it. So instead of consuming wholesome food, God's own blood-bought people were, in a spiritual sense, trying to feed on the wind. The wind is something which is illusory, something that cannot be grasped. In other words, instead of living in accordance with God's covenant, which alone could bring them lasting peace and satisfaction, they were hankering after something which seemed much more exciting. 'Just as the scorching east wind, like the Arabian sirocco, destroys plants and grass, so God was understood to destroy human pride (see Psalm 103:15-18; Jeremiah 4:11).' They were just like Hosea's wife, who had forsaken the love of her husband (which was strong and satisfying) and had turned aside to other lovers (who would only make use of her and then discard her). This is what was happening: Ephraim was trying to keep both Assyria and Egypt happy, but, like the wind, was vacillating between them both. While making a treaty with Assyria, Israel was also sending olive oil to Egypt.

Therefore, since both Ephraim and Judah need to be brought to their senses, God reminds them of the story of their common ancestor, Jacob. He did this because, although Jacob came to enjoy a living relationship with God, his early days were characterized by deceit. Before his encounters with God at Bethel and the brook Jabbok he behaved like the house of Israel were doing in Hosea's time. The story of his early years is filled with lies and deceit.

Jacob had a twin brother. His brother, Esau, emerged from his mother's womb first. This meant that in the ordinary course of events it would have been his place to be the heir to his father's property. But right from the beginning Jacob would not accept this. As Esau was delivered it was noticed that the tiny hand of Jacob was firmly gripping his brother's heel (12:3; Genesis 25:26). From that point onwards Jacob grew up to be deceptive and grasping. He tricked Esau out of his birthright. He deceived his blind old father into thinking he was the first-born son, so that he received his father's blessing, even though the old man suspected that something was not quite right.

Naturally Esau was not happy about this, and eventually Jacob had to flee from his brother's wrath, so he travelled away to the north, to his uncle Laban's home. But on the way he stopped for the night at Luz. There, in a dream, he saw a stairway reaching from the earth to heaven. Above it stood the Lord, who said to him, 'I am the LORD, the God of your father Abraham and the God of Isaac. I will give you and your descendants the land on which you are lying. Your descendants will be like the dust of the earth, and you will spread out to the west and to the east, to the north and to the south. All peoples on earth will be blessed through you and your offspring' (Genesis 28:13–14).

This was the same promise that had been given to his grandfather, Abraham. 'When Jacob awoke from his sleep, he thought, "Surely the LORD is in this place, and I was not aware of it"' (Genesis 28:16). So he renamed the place Bethel (which means, 'the house of God'). Therefore, although Jacob had been a deceiver, God met him and was gracious to him. Twenty years after this dream Jacob felt that it was high time to put matters right with his brother, so in fear and trepidation he returned to face Esau once again. He was naturally scared, after the way he had swindled Esau, but at the brook Jabbok a strange thing happened. The Bible tells us that Jacob wrestled with a man, who we later learn was God in the form of an angel (Genesis 32:24–32). Jacob struggled and, amazingly, overcame 'the man' but, realizing that it was none other than the Lord he was fighting against, he experienced deep sorrow for his sin and begged for God's favour (which is another word for grace).

In this passage Hosea is reminding the people that Jacob (deceitful though he had been) knew what it was to weep on account of his wrongdoing and in humility beg for God to show him his grace (12:4), and God did so. After this, Jacob was in a spiritual condition to meet his brother and make his peace with him. Obviously God had been working in Esau's heart, too, because he received Jacob kindly, despite what his younger brother had done to him.

Some time later God told Jacob, '"Go up to Bethel and settle there, and build an altar there to God, who appeared to you when you were fleeing from your brother Esau." So Jacob said to his household and to all who were with him, "Get rid of the foreign gods you have with you, and purify yourselves and change your clothes"' (Genesis 35:1–2). After this we read that 'God said to him, "Your name is Jacob, but you will no longer be called Jacob; your name will be Israel." So he named him Israel' (Genesis 35:10). Israel was the name given to the nation that grew out of Jacob's descendants, the people whom God brought out of Egypt—the very people to whom Hosea was ministering.

What has all this talk about Jacob to do with these people in Hosea's time, hundreds of years later? Simply this—he wanted to remind them that they were descendants of Jacob (in fact he calls them 'Jacob' in 12:2). They were just as deceitful as their forefather Jacob had been before his encounter with God at Bethel (12:4). But God was calling upon them to change their attitude and their lifestyle, as Jacob had done. Unless they repented of their sinfulness, God was going to punish them according to their ways and repay them according to their deeds (see 12:2). This is why he utters this heart-rending cry in verse 6: 'You must return to your God; maintain love and justice, and wait for your God always.' It is almost as if he says, 'I really can't bear the thought of what will happen to you if you don't repent and return to your God.'

This is a constant cry of all the prophets. Micah pleads with the people:

[God] has showed you, O man, what is good.
   And what does the Lord require of you?
To act justly and to love mercy
   and to walk humbly with your God   (Micah 6:8).

The message is clear: they had to amend their ways. This was the situation they were in: Bethel was no longer the house of God. It was now 'the house of wickedness', as we saw in 4:15. When the people of Hosea's day went there they did not find

God; they found a golden calf (10:5; 13:2). This was a shameful and sad state for the people to be in.

Shame in the present (12:7-8)

To reinforce his message Hosea points to the behaviour of the people, especially the merchants of Ephraim. The use of dishonest scales had been forbidden to God's people in Leviticus 19:36, yet the prophets continually had to call upon the people to obey God's Word and act honestly in regard to their neighbours. In Hebrew the word for 'merchant' sounds like the word 'Canaan'. God was telling his people that they were behaving just like the Canaanites whom their forefathers had been instructed to drive out of the land. However, those who love to defraud people of money or property do not mind whose laws they are breaking, so long as they get their own way. This is worldliness, and this is what Ephraim was guilty of. They were behaving just like the heathen people who were still living around them. They had the idea (which some people still have today) that the provision of great amounts of money is, of itself, a sign of God's blessing. But this is not necessarily the case; in fact, the rich person has to be very careful that his wealth does not corrupt him. Jesus said, 'It is easier for a camel to go through the eye of a needle than for a rich man to enter the kingdom of God' (Matthew 19:24). Lloyd Ogilvie wrote, 'A friend of mine who is a wealthy entrepreneur confided, "The power of money is intoxicating. It will get you anything you want from people except real love and will get you into any place except heaven."' He continued, 'The more you have, the closer you have to stay to God.'

Ephraim had failed to learn that lesson. The nation boasted: 'I am very rich; I have become wealthy. With all my wealth they will not find in me any iniquity or sin' (12:8). The Ephraimites were not saying that they had not sinned. What they were saying was: 'They will not find in me any iniquity or sin.' In other words, 'Because I am wealthy I can pay to have my wrongdoing covered up!' They were mistaken, of course. Sin will always become public—in the end. Throughout history many have discovered that even paying for the best lawyers to represent them in court has not always enabled them to avoid paying for the consequences of their sin.

If the merchants were using dishonest scales, who were being defrauded? It is always the poorest people of the land who fare the worst when corruption flourishes. Often the rich man makes his money at the cost of the underprivileged. For all his boasting, he will not escape on the day of reckoning.

This is a warning to us all. The book of Proverbs tells us, 'He who oppresses the poor shows contempt for their Maker, but whoever is kind to the needy honours God' (Proverbs 14:31). A. W. Tozer said, 'Honesty that can be trusted and respected is a very fragrant flower in the life of the Christian.'

Retribution in the future (12:9–14)

In the midst of Hosea's denunciation of the rich people comes the voice of God, thundering out, 'I am the LORD your God, who brought you out of Egypt.' The people are reminded who the real God is. It is not money or power or prestige (or Baal). The real God is the one who delivered them from the slavery of Egypt through the blood of the spotless Passover lamb. Following their deliverance they lived in the desert in tents, but they observed various religious feasts which reminded them of the blessing of their God upon them.

During the whole of their wanderings, and their life in the promised land, they were never left without God. He spoke to them through his prophets, and these godly men (and a few women) instructed them and guided them through the dangers of life. Hosea then takes the people back to the life of Jacob. During the many years their forefather spent with his uncle, Laban, he tended sheep. He became very good at it too! But he also learned what it was to be on the receiving end of deceit. Anything that he could do in that area, his uncle could do better. Jacob worked for seven years to marry Laban's beautiful daughter, Rachel (this was in lieu of a dowry), but he was deceived into marrying Leah! So he had to work for a further seven years to pay for Rachel.

Moses was the 'prophet' that God 'used to bring Israel up from Egypt' (12:13). He too had been a shepherd. He cared for Israel as lovingly as he had shepherded his flock. The implication here is that Hosea is also a prophet and the reason that he is giving the people all these warnings of future judgement is because he cares for them. He wants to lead them into good ways, as the other prophets before him had done.

How did the people respond to God's wise and gracious shepherding? They sacrificed bulls in Gilgal and they built altars all over the land (12:11; cf. 8:11). Hosea cries out for anyone who would listen, 'Is Gilead wicked?' Everyone knew the answer to that question. Of course it was (see 6:8–9). Here Gilead represents the people as a whole. They (or the vast majority of them) were 'worthless', so far as God was concerned, and their altars would soon be thrown down. Because they had provoked God to anger, they were going to be repaid for their contempt. They would be made to live in tents once again (12:9).

They were murderers (guilty of 'bloodshed', 12:14). Therefore, they would die because of their sin. Over and over again in the Bible the same message comes: the soul that sins shall die. So there was no hope for the northern kingdom of Israel. They had sinned grievously, and so they would have to be destroyed. God was going to use heathen Assyria to carry out his work.

But if they were all doomed, why did Hosea call upon them to return to their God? (12:6). It was because he was going to deal with them as individuals. Anyone who turns away from his, or her, sin and turns to God in humble faith, will be saved. However, God still requires blood to be shed for sin, but the only sacrifice of blood that he will accept is the blood of a sinless man. There is one who fulfils that requirement. The Lord Jesus Christ shed his precious blood upon the cross of Calvary in order to pay the price of anyone who will return to God.

This was the good news for Hosea's hearers, and it is the good news for the people of our day, too. Modern Western society is doomed because of its sinfulness. No one will be saved just by being a citizen of a 'Christian' country. God will only save those who come under conviction of their sin (as Jacob did). But for those who do genuinely repent and turn to Christ there is mercy.

20

The wages of sin

Please read Hosea 13:1–8

When the Israelite tribes eventually reached the borders of the promised land, the Gadites and the Reubenites went up to Moses and asked him, 'Can't we settle here, on the east side of Jordan? It's very suitable for our livestock.' Moses told them that they could have that region as their inheritance, but first of all they must go with the rest of the tribes and cross over the Jordan to fight against the nations who were currently occupying the land. If they refused to do this then they would be sinning against the Lord. Moses then added these well-known words: 'You may be sure that your sin will find you out' (Numbers 32:23).

Sin always has a way of rising to the surface. When we sit back and start to think that we are fine, upstanding people, then something happens to expose our wrongdoing. This was the kind of situation that the northern kingdom of Israel (Ephraim) found itself in as Hosea approached the end of his prophecy.

Ephraim, too, was in its final days. King Hoshea was on the throne. He was the last in a line of bad kings, all of whom led the people into idolatry and rebellion against God, instead of into the way of truth. Shalmaneser V was on the throne of their northern neighbour, Assyria. His kingdom had already occupied much of the land of Israel and was now waiting to pounce upon the rest of it. 2 Kings 17:5 tells us: 'The king of Assyria invaded the entire land, marched against Samaria and laid siege to it for three years.' This means that, as we commence looking at Hosea 13, things were looking very black indeed for Ephraim.

The destiny of Ephraim outlined (13:1-3)

As he speaks to the people, Hosea again takes them back into their past history. He reminds them that there was a time when they were a force to be reckoned with. Ephraim (the tribe who were descended from the second son of Joseph) was exalted in Israel: 'When Ephraim spoke, men trembled' (13:1). Many mighty men had come from the tribe of Ephraim, including Joshua (Numbers 13:8; Joshua 24:30), the great captain who took over the leadership of the nation when Moses died and who led the people into the promised land. However, as the proverb says, 'Pride goes before a fall' (see Proverbs 16:18). These victorious people of Ephraim became far too puffed up with a sense of their own importance. In their pride they became complacent and they did not take enough care of their spiritual lives.

We, too, must make sure that we do not become too proud of our achievements. We are not to serve God in the hope of constantly receiving a pat on the back for our efforts. If, with the ability God gives us, we do something well, we should be humble about it. Also we should hold other believers in greater esteem than ourselves (Philippians 2:3).

The problem with the people of Ephraim was that they became over-confident in their own abilities. They behaved as though they had no need of God, or of following in the ways of men of God such as Joshua. Instead they looked for encouragement elsewhere. In doing so, they fell into the very trap that God had warned them about many years beforehand.

In Deuteronomy 32 we read Moses' song. In it we have an account of how the nation would quickly fall away from the Lord and his commands. Moses calls Israel by the name Jeshurun, which means 'the upright one'. He speaks to them like this:

> Jeshurun grew fat and kicked;
>   filled with food, he became heavy and sleek.
> He abandoned the God who made him
>   and rejected the Rock his Saviour.
> They made him jealous with their foreign gods
>   and angered him with their detestable idols.
> They sacrificed to demons, which are not God—
>   gods they had not known,
>   gods that recently appeared,
>   gods your fathers did not fear.
> You deserted the Rock, who fathered you;
>   you forgot the God who gave you birth
>
> (Deuteronomy 32:15–18).

It is the same kind of thing that Hosea is reminding the people of here, at the beginning of chapter 13. Although they had once been well thought of among the nations, they had since fallen. This happened when they turned away from the God who loved them and had rescued them from the bondage of Egypt. They turned towards other gods, false gods. Hosea puts it very bluntly: 'He [Ephraim] became guilty of Baal worship.' In other words, the Ephraimites had broken the First Commandment. The consequence of this was that, as a nation, they 'died'.

The nation, or the individual, who deliberately turns away from the one true and living God is spiritually dead. Paul tells the Ephesians that, before Christ found them and saved them, they were 'dead in ... transgressions and sins' (Ephesians 2:1). That is what life is like for the unsaved. They are separated from God as a result of their sins. So far as the Lord is concerned, they are dead spiritually, just as one day they will be dead physically.

Hosea then gives the people an outline of their sinful ways. They did more than just worship the Baals. They made idols for themselves from their silver, and they set their craftsmen to work on fashioning these images (13:2; cf. 8:4). Through these actions they also broke the Second Commandment.

It is not clear from this passage whether these people actually offered human sacrifices, but they evidently had a reputation of being the kind of people who would do such things (see also 2 Kings 17:17; 23:10). Also when they came to Bethel (or any other place where there were images of the golden calf-god), they bowed down to the idols and kissed them. Kissing the idol was evidently a regular part of Baal-worship in the time of Elijah (1 Kings 19:18). What does a kiss indicate? It is a sign of love and affection, or a pledge of loyalty to the sovereign or some other ruler. These people, who claimed to be the people of God, were kissing a calf, an idol.

God had told them that they should 'kiss the Son, lest he be angry and you be destroyed in your way' (Psalm 2:12). This Son is the one who blesses 'all who take refuge in him'. Surely, then, this psalm is a foretelling of the Lord Jesus Christ. But these people had fallen so far away from God and his Word that there was only one course open to the Lord in dealing with them. He was going to destroy them. In fact, he tells them that they have died already. They are quickly going to fade away.

He gives them four illustrations to show them what would happen to them, unless they repented.

First, he says that 'They will be like the morning mist, like the early dew that disappears' (13:3). They well knew that, as soon as the sun came up, its warmth would cause the mist and dew to disappear and melt away into the atmosphere. This was what would happen to the people because of their sinfulness. They would not be able to stand before the intense heat of the fire of God's judgement. Malachi 3:2 poses the question: 'Who can endure the day of his [the Lord Jesus Christ's] coming? Who can stand when he appears?' Jesus has already come to bring salvation into the world, but we must remember that he is coming again one day. This time he will judge the ungodly.

To reinforce the image, Hosea uses two more pictures. He tells them that on the Day of Judgement they will be 'like chaff swirling from a threshing-floor'. The farmer wants the wind to blow away this useless part of his crop.

The final illustration is of 'smoke escaping through a window'. In the kind of houses they had in those days, a window would simply have been an opening, one of the purposes of which would have been to let out the smoke from the hearth.

That is the kind of thing that was certainly going to happen to Ephraim. On the Day of Judgement they would be utterly destroyed. The Assyrians, with the permission of God, were ready to carry out the utter devastation of Israel, as we shall see in the second half of this chapter. As a nation, Ephraim was about to be destroyed—unless they returned to their God.

When we come to look at 13:14 we shall see that there is hope of resurrection for those who are dead spiritually, but who put their trust in God and forsake their sinful ways. But before we come to that passage we see that God does not give up on them entirely. Instead he shows them once more what kind of God he is.

The power of God displayed (13:4–8)

Once again the Lord reminds the Israelites of who he is and what he has done for them. He refreshes their memory once again: 'I am the LORD your God, who brought you out of Egypt.' He wants them to stop thinking about what they are doing in the present. His desire is that they should look back to the Lord's past dealings with them. Surely, one who has done so much for them is worthy of love and obedience! It ought not to be difficult for them to walk in the ways of righteousness. He reminds them of his uniqueness. There is no God but the Lord, nor is there any other Saviour. If only they had kept the first commandment given to them through Moses on Mount Sinai they would not be in such danger. They had certainly proved over and over again that all the other gods of the Canaanites were worthless and ineffectual against their enemies.

God was not only unique; he was one who cared for them. Throughout those forty long years of wandering in the desert the Lord had kept them safe. He had provided food for them and all that was necessary for the maintenance of life and health. Yet see how they treated him for his kindness: they became proud and forgot him.

That is just what people do when things are going well with them. Sometimes hard-working wives say to their husbands, 'You take me for granted!' They usually add something about slaving over a hot oven all day and keeping the place neat and tidy. It is certainly true that a great many husbands do take their wives' love and care for granted.

Israel were proud to be called the people of God, yet they forgot him and failed to keep his laws. This is why God told them that he would devour them. He describes the coming judgement in terms of attacks by wild animals. These were fearsome encounters. He would deal with them in the most fearful ways. He would act like a lion, or a leopard lurking by the path. He would behave as a bear does when she is robbed of her cubs. There would be terrible punishment brought upon the house of Israel.

How can a God of love even contemplate doing such things to his people? Did he not say, 'How can I give you up, Ephraim? How can I hand you over, Israel?' (11:8). So how do the words of verses 7 and 8 tie up with the concept of a loving, caring God? It comes about because 'His love sometimes requires that he express his wrath.' In these verses we have an example of chastising love. This is the love of a father who punishes his son in order to bring him to his senses. In Hebrews 12:6 we read, 'The Lord disciplines those he loves, and he punishes everyone he accepts as a son.' Or as the seventeenth-century writer Samuel Butler put it: 'Spare the rod, and spoil the child.' God prefers to deal with his people by means of his Word, but if they refuse to listen, then he has to use more painful ways of bringing them back to himself and his ways.

The need for us to obey God's Word in our days
We may not be bowing down to images made of burnished metal, but are we really worshipping God? We, too, can become guilty of thinking all is well with us spiritually when that is far from being the case. We congratulate ourselves that we read our Bibles and pray to God every day, yet do we do this wholeheartedly and humbly? We should not let anything at all come between us and our God. We may justly be proud of our achievements and those of our children, but are we omitting to praise God for giving us the ability to accomplish these things?

A second question for us to consider is: 'Are we giving greater love to anyone, or anything, than we are to the Lord who loved us and gave himself for us?' Do we praise God for stooping down and rescuing us from the sin and degradation of this world? Before we came to the Christ of the cross we were dead in transgressions and sins, but he saw us in that state and he sent someone to preach the gospel to us so that we might come to the Saviour, confess our sins and be saved.

21

Where is your king?

Please read Hosea 13:9–16

E very organization needs a leader. Without someone to head up a work it is sure to run into problems. Even in a democracy it is vital to have good leaders. What country can succeed for long without a strong prime minister or president? Not everyone will like the person who is appointed to the post, but most people will agree that a project, or company, or country, is only going to succeed if it has a sound leader.

When the Israelites came out of the desert, after their forty years of wandering, they had someone at their head. Moses had guided them during those years, and Joshua succeeded him and led them into the promised land. These were godly men who leaned hard upon the Lord God Almighty to give them the power to act wisely and well. But as time went by the people became restless. They had their religious leaders, the prophets, but they wanted to be like the other countries around them—they wanted a king of their own.

There were three reasons why they wanted a king. Firstly, they thought that if they had their own king they would have stable, continuous government. Secondly, they assumed that they would be on equal terms with the other nations, who all had kings. Thirdly, they would have leadership in time of war. In other words, they thought that they would be better off if they turned to the countries around them for their inspiration (which meant turning away from God). They behaved just as Gomer did when she turned her back on her true and loving husband, who had provided for her needs, and turned aside to other, more exciting, lovers.

Despite the imminent danger they were in, the people of this northern kingdom of Israel were still turning away from that which was right and true, and turning towards the system of the world, thinking that their needs would be met there.

The rejection of God as King (13:9-13)
Back in the time of Samuel the people of Israel had asked for a king and princes. One day they came to the prophet and said, 'You are old, and your sons do not walk in your ways; now appoint a king to lead us, such as all the other nations have' (1 Samuel 8:5). Samuel was very displeased to hear this. Hosea tells us that God was angry too (13:11). Nevertheless the Lord did give them a king. That was in about the year 1031 BC. He gave them Saul, who at first sight appeared to be a godly man. Yet eventually he showed his true colours and disobeyed God's Word. So the Lord removed him from office. In his place he appointed King David, who was to head up a kingdom which would have no end.

However, things failed to go smoothly for Israel. There came a time when the kingdom was divided. The people of the northern part (called Israel, or Ephraim) chose a man called Jeroboam to be their king (1 Kings 12:20). He later came to be known as

Jeroboam I. The Bible does not tell us that the people sought guidance from God in making this choice, or that of subsequent kings. This is one of the complaints made against them in Hosea. God says, '[Israel] set up kings without my consent; they choose princes without my approval' (8:4).

It was Jeroboam who set up the two golden calves. One was at Dan (in the north), and the other was at Bethel (in the south). The idea of these calves was to discourage the people from going to Jerusalem to worship the Lord (1 Kings 12:27–29). Jerusalem was in the southern kingdom of Judah, and Jeroboam was afraid that the people would defect to that kingdom if they went there to worship. Jeroboam was the first in a line of twenty kings. Each one of these did that which was evil in God's sight. The best that could be said of any of them was that some were worse than others.

So, just as God gave Israel a king in his anger, he took the last king away in his wrath. In Hosea 13:9 God speaks directly to the people. Probably by this time the Assyrian king, Shalmaneser V, had already taken Hoshea (the last king of Israel) captive. We know that this happened in 725 BC. This may well be why God calls to the people and says, 'Where is your king?' He means, 'Where is this one upon whom you placed all your hopes?' The answer was that he had been removed into Assyrian exile. Therefore, God taunted them and said:

> Where is your king, that he may save you?
>> Where are your rulers in all your towns,
> of whom you said,
>> 'Give me a king and princes'?   (13:10).

We read about these events in 2 Kings 17:1–5. In other words, God's own people turned against him, the one who describes himself as their 'helper' (13:9).

Although God was their Sovereign Ruler and powerful Lord, he calls himself their helper. Three times in the Bible God is described in this way. He is the helper of the fatherless (Psalm 10:14); he is the helper of those who deserve God's punishment (Psalm 30:10); and he is the helper of those who are being pursued by their enemies (Psalm 54:4).

However, the people of the northern kingdom refused to look to the Lord, their helper. Nor did they recognize the dire situation they were in. They could not believe that God, their helper, was actually going to destroy them. They were so deadened by their sin that they failed to understand that they were acting against their own God. But God himself tells them that 'The guilt of Ephraim is stored up, his sins are kept on record.' Earlier Hosea had told them the same thing: 'God will remember their wickedness and punish them for their sins' (9:9). In Deuteronomy 32 God speaks about the folly of his people and says that he has sealed up the record of their sins in his vaults (Deuteronomy 32:34); and in Revelation John tells us, 'I saw the dead, great and small, standing before the throne, and books were opened ... The dead were judged according to what they had done as recorded in the books' (Revelation 20:12).

God was telling Israel the same thing in Hosea 13:12. One day their sins would be revealed and they would be weighed in the balances and found wanting—just as Belshazzar was in Daniel 5:27. Here in 13:9 we find God's judgement recorded: 'You are destroyed, O Israel, because you are against me ...' Destruction will come upon everyone who continues to be against the Lord and his Word.

Great pain was going to come upon Israel. This pain would be like the agonies of a woman in childbirth, but instead of this birth being followed by great joy, it would only result in anguish. This was because the child would not come to the opening of the womb. In those days such a condition would have resulted in the death of both the mother and the child. God tells them that this 'child' is 'without wisdom'—it is dead! In other words, because they, the people of God, were acting unwisely in not following the Lord, they could expect nothing but death and tears to follow them. That is the judgement that God pronounced on Israel. However, even though the Lord was angry with them, we can see God's love shining through. We remember that earlier he said, 'How can I give you up, Ephraim? How can I hand you over, Israel?' (11:8).

What does all this mean? It will help us understand if we look at Deuteronomy 4:27, where we read, 'The LORD will scatter you among the peoples, and only a few of you will survive among the nations to which the LORD will drive you.' So we see clearly taught in the earlier part of the Bible the fact that there will be a remnant who are still faithful to the Lord. These people will survive this dreadful judgement.

The promise of new life (13:14)

This northern kingdom of Israel was certainly going to be destroyed, and history tells us that this actually came to pass. They were about to go down into the grave. In 13:1 it is recorded that Ephraim had died. A dead body needs to be buried in a grave. Psalm 18:4–5 gives us an awful description of the grave:

> The cords of death entangled me;
> the torrents of destruction overwhelmed me.
> The cords of the grave coiled around me;
> the snares of death confronted me.

It is a place of cold and deadness. We all shiver when we think of graves. The psalmist tells us that 'The dead praise not the LORD, neither any that go down into silence' (Psalm 115:17, AV). So just as God has brought the people to think about the solemn realities and finality of the grave, he also thunders out this remarkable statement: 'I will ransom them from the power of the grave; I will redeem them from death.'

This is something that God was going to do with his own almighty power. The psalmist picks up the same theme: 'You will not abandon me to the grave' (Psalm 16:10). Something tremendous is promised to those who remain faithful to the Lord: they are going to be born again. They are going to receive new life. But we might say, 'Surely they don't deserve this, because they have behaved so abominably? They have turned aside from the Lord and his ways, and have turned to serve other gods. Is God just going to overlook their evil and forgive them because he has changed his mind about destroying them?' God's answer is: 'Certainly not.' He cannot do that because he is not dishonest.

Instead of destroying those who are faithful to his Word, he is going to 'ransom' them; he is going to 'redeem' them. Both of these words speak about the payment of a great price. Jesus said, 'The Son of Man did not come to be served, but to serve, and to give his life as a ransom for many' (Mark 10:45). The Israelites would have remembered how the blood of a pure young lamb, which was sprinkled upon the doorposts and lintels of their houses, had set their forefathers free from Egypt. This lamb had to be without spot or blemish, and it was slain to set them free, or redeem them, from their slavery (see Exodus 6:6).

The Passover lamb and these words from Hosea both point us forward to the death of the Lord Jesus Christ on the cross of Calvary. God's own spotless, sinless Lamb was sacrificed for the redemption of his people. His life was the ransom price paid to free his believing people from their sin. But, just as Jesus died, and was buried in the tomb, so we have to die because of our sin. We deserve to die, but he never did anything wrong.

Nevertheless he offered his life as a ransom for our sin. Then, on the third day, he rose again from the dead. Paul quotes Hosea 13:14 when he asks, 'Where, O death, is your victory? Where, O death, is your sting?' He immediately answers these questions by saying, 'The sting of death is sin, and the power of sin is the law.' He concludes: 'But thanks be to God! He gives us the victory through our Lord Jesus Christ' (1 Corinthians 15:55–57). Christ has won the victory over death and the grave. His Father did not abandon him to the grave, nor let his Holy One see decay (Psalm 16:10).

That same victory over death and the grave is offered to all who will come to Christ in simple and humble faith. It ought to have made the Israelites very excited to know that God was going to come and bring them, as a nation (or rather the remnant of their nation), back to life again. But observe how they reacted when they heard this good news.

The people without a king (13:14–16)

Although the Assyrians were nearby, and the defeat of Samaria was a foregone conclusion in the opinion of almost everyone, Ephraim was still proud. In their own eyes, the Ephraimites were thriving. The trouble was that they were living in the past! They were remembering the days when men had trembled at the voice of Ephraim and he was exalted in Israel (13:1).

Even though the name Ephraim meant 'fruitful', the northern kingdom was no longer flourishing; it was doomed. God was going to have no compassion upon its inhabitants. They would be taken away captive to Assyria. A strong 'east wind from the LORD will come, blowing in from the desert' (13:15). There is no doubt that this powerful east wind is the nation of Assyria, who would wreak even more havoc upon them than the strong desert wind. The result would be that Ephraim's 'spring will fail and his well dry up'.

In other words, Ephraim would find no further sustenance or blessing. Even 'his storehouse will be plundered of all its treasures'. It was on these treasures that the people had set their hearts. Jesus said, 'Where your treasure is, there your heart will be also' (Matthew 6:21).

That was what Assyria was going to do to them. And that is what God's judgement will bring upon all those who go on rejecting him and his salvation until the end of their days. Like the people of Samaria, they are going to have to bear their guilt because they have rebelled against their God.

Dreadful things were going to happen, even to the women and children of the land (see 2 Kings 15:16). This all came about because they had rebelled against their God. They had rejected their true King, the Lord God Almighty, and as a consequence they were about to be destroyed. They were going to have to bear the penalty for their own sins, because they had rejected God's offer of mercy.

There are so many people like that today. Christ, when he hung and suffered and died upon the cross of Calvary, won the victory over death and the grave. However, many people forget that the wages of sin is still death. The people of Samaria were so very foolish in rejecting God and his Word. So is anyone else who behaves like that. The only thing in store for them is also punishment—a castigation far worse than that endured by Israel in Assyria. It is the awful retribution described by Jesus, and called 'hell', where there is only weeping and gnashing of teeth. But just as the people of Samaria had the opportunity to repent, so does anyone who will turn to Jesus Christ and be saved.

This message also has meaning for those of us who have sought and found refuge in Christ. It helps us to realize the enormity of the punishment that might have been ours except for the sacrifice of our Lord, 'and the immensity of the love that has saved us'. It ought to fill our hearts with grateful, thankful praise.

22

Will you walk or stumble?

Please read Hosea 14:1–9

Many years ago I remember driving from Yorkshire to Lancashire and ending up driving up and down the streets of Manchester. I was looking for a signpost that would show me the way *out* of the city, but whichever road I took, I always found myself heading back once again for the city centre.

We do not even need to be in a large city to get lost. It can happen to us just as easily in the countryside when we are flanked by nothing but trees and fields. We keep driving until we come to a T-junction and we are relieved when we see a signpost there with writing on it. But when we arrive all we learn is that if we go to the left it will take us to Little Drinkwater and if we turn to the right we shall end up in Much-Snoring-in-the-Dell—when the only thing we want to know is: 'How can I find the road that leads me back to London?'

Life is so often like that. We are caught not knowing where

to go, and we want to find our way home to satisfaction and peace. Then when we arrive at a crossroads we are offered two choices, but the problem is that we do not know which one to take. However, when it comes to the teaching of the Bible, there is absolutely no doubt as to which is the best way to go.

Near the end of the book of Joshua, that great leader of God's people faced them with one of two choices. He urged them to 'Fear the LORD and serve him with all faithfulness' (Joshua 24:14). He told them that if they did so then they would have to throw away the gods their forefathers had worshipped beyond the River and in Egypt. They would need to serve the Lord only. Then he gave them an alternative: 'But if serving the LORD seems undesirable to you, then choose for yourselves this day whom you will serve, whether the gods your forefathers served beyond the River, or the gods of the Amorites, in whose land you are living.'

He gave them a straight choice. They could either serve the one true and living God, or they could choose to worship the false gods, which included both those which their forefathers had served in Egypt and the gods of the people of the land— gods like the Baals. Joshua was not forcing them to do what he wanted; he just set the two choices before them. But then he told them what he was going to do. He said, 'But as for me and my household, we will serve the LORD' (Joshua 24:14). At the time the people were unanimous in giving their wholehearted assent to serving the Lord, but as time passed they became more integrated with the gods of the land and they commenced worshipping the Baals instead of the true God.

So, as we come to the last of our studies in the prophecy of Hosea, we are going to see God putting before the people the same choice as Joshua put before their forefathers. He says that those who obey the Lord and serve him will make a wise choice;

they will succeed in every way. However, those who rebel against God and his Word will make a foolish choice, and they will stumble. And in doing so they will not merely graze their legs; they will end up under the judgement of God in the place of eternal punishment and suffering.

The last verse in Hosea is rather like Psalm 1, which tells us about the way of the righteous and the way of the wicked.

Genuine repentance (14:1–3)

Back at the beginning of Hosea chapter 6 we saw that the people seemed to be repenting of their sins, but their show of sorrow came to nothing because it was only a half-hearted attempt at repentance. However, here we see genuine repentance at work. This is how we can know that their sorrow was sincere. They demonstrated that they had listened to the words of Hosea. They showed that they had recognized that he spoke God's words to them, and they knew that these words were appropriate for them at that particular time in their history.

Therefore, this time they were determined to be more sensible; they were going to listen. They were going to be sincere in their desire to return to the Lord, and they were going to serve him to the very best of their abilities.

In the first three verses of Hosea 14 God tells the people of Israel what they ought to do.

1. They had to admit that they had been wrong (14:1)

This is not an easy thing to do. None of us likes to admit our failure, but that was exactly what God required of them. They had to acknowledge that their sins had been their downfall, and they had to accept that the only hope for them was to return to the Lord their God.

This is a vital message for all of us today. If we are going to experience the peace of God in our hearts and lives then we have to repent of our sins. The first step in that process is to admit to ourselves, and then to God, that we have done wrong.

2. They had to confess their sins and seek God's forgiveness (14:2)

They had to return to the Lord and speak sincere words of repentance. They were not to come to God seeking to justify, or make excuses for, their wrongdoing. They were not to bring words of rebellion, impertinent demands, or proud self-righteousness. They were to bring words of repentant faith. In Jeremiah 3:22 the people said to God, 'We will come to you, for you are the LORD our God.' Instead of animal sacrifices, the only offerings that the Lord would find acceptable were the fruit of their lips—in other words, sincere words of genuine repentance. God wants all of us to behave in just that same way today.

3. They had to turn back to God (14:3)

This was no easy thing for them. In turning back to God they had to confess that they had done so many things unwisely, and had been wrong in the past. They had tried turning to two strong nations for help—Assyria and Egypt. But they had to admit, from their own bitter experience, that these powers could not help them. Also at one time they had put their trust in strong war-horses. Yet these instruments of war had not saved them either. Finally they had to accept that idols made by their own craftsmen were not gods at all, nor could they bring blessing to them and their crops.

In the light of this humbling experience they may well have felt forsaken, especially as they had the Assyrian threat hanging over them. But this is where we see the graciousness of God. If only they returned to the Lord they would discover that, although they were like orphans, their God would be a Father to them.

In Hosea 13:14 God had told them that he would have no compassion upon them. This was because they were proud and heading away from him, but when once they returned to him in sincerity and truth, Hosea tells them that they would experience his deep compassion and love.

When we are seeking blessing where do we go for it? Do we follow the example of the world and seek it in sound investments, in pleasures and in furious activity? Rather than turning to such things, we ought to do what Israel finally did. Instead of these things holding centre stage in our lives, we should come and in humility admit our failure, confess our sin and turn to the Lord, because he alone can save us. In an attempt to reach this state we should ask ourselves questions like: 'What things have been my downfall?' and 'Do these things draw me nearer to God, or drive me further from him?'

True forgiveness (14:4–8)

When once the people had admitted their faults, confessed their sins and returned to the Lord, then he promised to heal their waywardness and love them freely. Repentance brings about a complete transformation in our lives. One of the tests we can use to see if we are genuine Christians is to ask ourselves questions along these lines: 'Has there been a radical change in my life? Am I different from before I came to Christ? Are my values now those of Christ, and not those of the world around me?'

Verse 4 shows us the wonderful grace of God in action. He had said to these people, 'I will no longer love them' (9:15), but now he says, 'I will ... love them freely' (14:4). What has brought about the change? It is their desire to turn away from the false gods, and turn to the one true and living God. This is the theme of this entire book. God has been at work. Although Israel did not deserve it, he had said, 'I am ... going to allure her ... and speak tenderly to her' (2:14). He had also said:

> I will plant her for myself in the land;
>   I will show my love to the one I called 'Not my loved one'.
> I will say to those called 'Not my people', 'You are my people';
>   and they will say, 'You are my God'   (2:23).

Now he says, 'My anger has turned away from them' (14:4). In other words, 'Because they have repented (i.e. turned away from evil and turned towards the living God), I will now love them and turn away my anger from them.'

In most of the earlier chapters of this book we have been looking at hardly anything but the doom and gloom to be unleashed upon these people because of their sinfulness. Now a wonderful ray of sunlight has burst upon the scene. God is no longer angry with them. But does this mean that he has changed his mind about sin? No, it does not. What it means is that the penalty of sin has been paid, not by these sinners, but by another. The one who paid the price of sin is God's only begotten Son, the Lord Jesus Christ. It is true that another several hundred years were going to pass before he was to be born on this earth, yet his death has turned away God's fierce anger, and everyone who turns away from their sin in genuine repentance will receive God's true forgiveness. It is all because of Christ's atoning death on the cross of Calvary.

In verses 5–8 Hosea goes on to tell them of the blessings that God will bring upon them because they have turned back to him in genuine repentance and faith. He uses agricultural terms, because they would have understood exactly what he meant. However, he is speaking here of spiritual realities. He is comparing their new spiritual lives to plants growing and producing wonderful flowers and fruit.

When Israel had been revived and reconciled to God they were going to bring great honour to God's name and great blessing to others.

1. They were going to bring freshness
The dew of God was going to come upon them and they would bring forth beauty and fragrance like lilies and cedar trees. They were going to bring the blessings of shade from the fierce heat of the sun.

2. They were going to provide stability
They were not going to be shallow-rooted like the lily. They were going to have long, firm roots like the wonderful cedar trees of Lebanon.

3. They were going to have great vigour
They were going to produce young shoots, which would grow and reach ever outwards. As God had promised their father Abraham, he would make of them 'a great nation ... and all peoples on earth [would] be blessed' through them (see Genesis 12:2, 3). They would flourish like corn and produce many grains of new corn from a single seed which had been planted in the ground in the springtime.

God ends this section with a cry. In verse 8 he says, 'O Ephraim, what more have I to do with idols?' This is similar to David's cry over the death of his wayward son Absalom: 'O my son Absalom! My son, my son Absalom! If only I had died instead of you—O Absalom, my son, my son!' (2 Samuel 18:33). It is also like the cry of Jesus over self-righteous Jerusalem: 'O Jerusalem, Jerusalem, you who kill the prophets and stone those sent to you, how often I have longed to gather your children together, as a hen gathers her chicks under her wings, but you were not willing' (Matthew 23:37).

God finally cries out for them to have done with idols for

ever, and he reminds them that they would be fruitful in the land. They would live out the meaning of the name 'Ephraim'. But they must always remember that their fruitfulness comes from the Lord. It is all of grace. They do not deserve it. It is not through their own efforts. It is by the grace of God, and for his honour, that they are fruitful.

A challenge (14:9)

Who is wise enough to understand the message of Hosea and to act upon it? Proverbs 9:10 tells us, 'The fear of the LORD is the beginning of wisdom, and knowledge of the Holy One is understanding.' How can we get that wisdom from God? We obtain it by listening to what he says, and obeying his Word. Jesus constantly told his hearers, 'He that has ears to hear, let him hear.'

The message of the prophets is that those who turn from their wicked ways and turn to God will be saved. Look at the Word of God. Look at godly people around you and you see that they walk in the ways of the Lord. The other way leads to death. Throughout this book the concept of 'stumbling' has often been spoken about (e.g. 4:5; 5:5). Those who fall will one day find that they do not have the strength to get up again. One day sin will get the better of those who continue in those ways.

We do not know how the people of Hosea's time responded to his message, but we do know how we are going to respond. We are either going to turn around and turn towards God, or we are going to continue in our foolish ways.

Obadiah

An introduction to Obadiah

While the prophecy of Hosea is full of tender longing for Israel to return to the Lord, this small book of Obadiah takes a totally different tack. It is similar in that its message is aimed at those who have turned their back on the one true and living God and his people. Yet it is very different in the sense that it is full of violent language concerning judgement upon those who have continually shown an 'unbrotherly' attitude towards the people of God.

Here we have details of the vision which God gave to a prophet about the country of Edom. We know nothing else about the man except that his name means 'servant (or worshipper) of the LORD.' There are some twelve people called Obadiah elsewhere in the Old Testament (see 1 Kings 18:3-16; 1 Chronicles 3:21; 7:3; 8:38; 9:16; 12:9; 27:19; 2 Chronicles 17:7; 34:12; Ezra 8:9; Nehemiah 10:5; 12:25). Neither the name of the prophet's father nor his place of birth is given.

The date and place of this prophecy are disputed. The only clue to the time of writing is the mention of the destruction of

Jerusalem (v. 11). There are two specific events in Israel's history to which this could refer.

First, there was the invasion of Jerusalem by Philistines and Arabs during the reign of Jehoram (853-841 BC—see 2 Kings 8:20-22; 2 Chronicles 21:8-20). If this is the period mentioned in verses 11-12 then Obadiah would have been a contemporary of Elisha.

The other occasion was the Babylonian attacks on Jerusalem (605-586 BC). If these are the events referred to, Obadiah would have been a contemporary of Jeremiah. In this commentary we shall assume that this is the more likely date. One of the strongest reasons for dating the prophecy in the sixth century BC would be the parallels between Obadiah 1-9 and Jeremiah 49:7-22. Some scholars believe that there was some kind of interdependence between Obadiah and Jeremiah, but it may be that both prophets were drawing on a common source not otherwise known to us.

The theme of the prophecy is that of Edom. This mountain kingdom had always been very proud of its security. Edom's hostile activities had spanned the centuries of Israel's existence. As we commence to examine this small and rather neglected prophecy, we shall notice how significant a place it occupies in the plan of God for his people.

We now leave Hosea and the eighth century BC and move onwards some two hundred years. We also turn our attention away from the northern part of the land and look far to the south of Samaria, to the mountainous area that borders the Dead Sea.

23

Pride goes before destruction

Please read Obadiah 1–9

Obadiah's message was given to the people of Judah, but it concerned their southern neighbour, Edom. The land of Edom was the very mountainous area that lay to the south-east of the Dead Sea. Through Obadiah God made the solemn announcement that he was calling on the nations around to rise up against the country of Edom, and 'go against her for battle' (v. 1).

God never says such things lightly. He is a God of love. Jesus tells us to love our enemies (Matthew 5:44). However, God will vindicate his name and his truth. The Edomites had been constant enemies of Israel. They were descended from Esau. He sold his birthright to his younger twin brother, Jacob, for a meal of red stew (Genesis 25:27–34). The name 'Esau' actually means 'red' and it is interesting to note that the rocks of Edom (the land where Esau's descendants dwelt) were also red.

Jacob later secured his father's blessing which, tradition

dictated, should have gone to the elder son, Esau (Genesis 27). The act provoked a conflict between the two brothers, and this hatred spread to the two nations that sprang from them. We have an example of this continuing animosity when the Israelites sought permission to enter the promised land by passing through Edom. The Edomites were adamant in refusing to allow them to do so, even though the Israelites promised not to harm their land in any way (Numbers 20:14–21).

Obadiah is the shortest book in the Old Testament, and it is seldom preached upon. It is not quoted directly in the New Testament. However, verse 21 declares, 'The kingdom will be the LORD's' and this is echoed in Revelation 11:15, where we read, 'The kingdom of the world has become the kingdom of our Lord and of his Christ, and he will reign for ever and ever.'

But just because the prophecy is short, and deals only with judgement upon the little country of Edom, that does not mean that we can ignore it. Paul said that 'All Scripture is God-breathed and is useful for teaching, rebuking, correcting and training in righteousness, so that the man of God may be thoroughly equipped for every good work' (2 Timothy 3:16–17). Therefore, because this little book is in the Bible, it must have something useful to say to us.

The pride of Edom
God spoke against these people for many reasons and they can all be summed up in this one word, 'pride'. God tells us that he hates 'pride and arrogance' (Proverbs 8:13). He says, 'Pride only breeds quarrels, but wisdom is found in those who take advice' (Proverbs 13:10). He also tells us that 'Pride goes before destruction, a haughty spirit before a fall' (Proverbs 16:18). The Lord was going to destroy this nation because they were proud and arrogant. They fought against God's will just as

their forefather had done when he refused to serve his younger brother (see Genesis 25:23).

These people were proud for a number of reasons.

1. They were proud because of their isolation
They occupied high ground. They could easily defend their cities, which could only be approached by narrow gullies coming up from the plains. Those who have visited the ruins of ancient Petra will know how grand and magnificent these cities were.

Because they lived high up in the mountains, and thus could overlook every other nation, they thought they could manage without God. Scholars tell us that there is no indication that the Edomites worshipped any God—not even the Baals, or any idol of wood or stone. They felt themselves to be so secure that they did not need anyone outside of themselves. The psalmist tells us that 'In his pride the wicked does not seek [the LORD]; in all his thoughts there is no room for God' (Psalm 10:4). So many people suffer from this attitude of self-sufficiency today. They think they do not need God, or anyone else to help them. They forget that one day they are going to have to stand before the one who judges all things.

God said to Edom, 'The pride of your heart has deceived you … you who say to yourself, "Who can bring me down to the ground" ' (v. 3). They were going to discover that there was one who would crush them. God was going to make sure that they were cut down to size, but he was going to do so in his own good time. He says that they 'will be cut down in the slaughter' (v. 9).

2. They were proud because of the strength of their homes
These were built way up in the rock, some 3,800 feet (1,150 metres) above sea level. This made them difficult for an enemy to reach, and so they felt secure. However, even though a natural enemy might find it difficult to reach them, they were not out

of God's reach. He addressed them as 'You who live in the clefts of the rocks and make your home on the heights' (v. 3), and told them they were going to be destroyed:

> 'Though you soar like the eagle
>   and make your nest among the stars,
>   from there I will bring you down,'
>   declares the LORD   (v. 4).

No one can escape from the Lord. Jonah discovered this when he tried to run away from the work that God had called him to do. He ended up inside the great fish, and, ultimately, he still had to go to Nineveh and call its people to repentance.

3. They were proud because they were prosperous
Their country lay on the trade routes between India and Egypt, and also from the northern countries. The trade which they carried out with passing merchants had made them very rich, and they made sure that they kept their treasures safe by hiding them high up in secret caves (see v. 6). They were also wealthy because the mountain slopes were ideal for growing grapes. With the money which they collected for trade and from agriculture they had become very rich, and they put great trust in this fortune. But they failed to grasp the fact that amassing huge sums of money cannot help anyone when it comes to facing a God who is angry at arrogance and pride.

4. They were proud because they had alliances with the nations around them
They made pacts with everyone—except with Judah. They relied on the support of the nations. They were so proud that they would not depend on the Lord God Almighty to help them. The psalmist tells us:

> It is better to take refuge in the LORD
>   than to trust in man.

It is better to take refuge in the LORD
    than to trust in princes   (Psalm 118:8–9).

5. They were proud because of the wise men in their midst
They assumed that the wisdom of men is better than the wisdom of God. They did not know that God has said, 'Do not be wise in your own eyes; fear the LORD and shun evil' (Proverbs 3:7). They were so foolish as to think that they could trust in human wisdom. Proverbs 11:2 tells us, 'When pride comes, then comes disgrace, but with humility comes wisdom.'

Taking all this into account, we can see that these rugged, self-sufficient people of Edom were far off from God. This is the reason for Obadiah's prophecy. The people of Judah had been humiliated by the Edomites time and time again, and more recently they had seen their beloved city of Jerusalem ransacked by the Babylonians. What action did the people of nearby Edom take when this happened? Obadiah tells us that they 'stood aloof' (v. 11).

The prophet tells us what God was going to do about the pride of Edom.

God's judgement on Edom
No individual, or nation, can succeed for ever in ridiculing God and his people. They may get away with it for very many years, but in the end they will be punished. The whole of this little book is about what God is going to do to Edom.

1. He is going to mobilize the surrounding nations and 'go against her for battle' (v. 1).

2. He is going to make them small (v. 2); he is going to cut them down to size (v. 9). They may behave as though they are free to soar up into the heights like the powerful, magnificent eagle, but they are going to discover that God is even more

exalted than the eagle. In the end he will bring them down (v. 4) and utterly humiliate them.

When the people tried to build the tower of Babel they said, 'Come, let us build ourselves a city, with a tower that reaches to the heavens, so that we may make a name for ourselves and not be scattered over the face of the whole earth' (Genesis 11:4). But because of their pride the Lord punished them. They stopped building and they were scattered throughout the world. That is why we have to learn foreign languages today.

3. God is going to destroy them and their possessions. He reminds them of what happens when thieves arrive at night. He says they take your things and they pick your grapes (v. 5), and they cause a great deal of distress and hardship. But when the time comes for them to leave they only take what they can carry. They leave behind a few things and some grapes on the vines. The Lord points out to them that, awful as that kind of thing is, when he comes upon them in judgement it will be far worse: he will completely ransack everything that belongs to them, and there will be nothing left behind! In effect he says to them, 'I know where you have hidden your precious stones and metal because nothing can be hidden from my sight.'

God has all-seeing eyes. Jesus tells us that when God comes in judgement, 'There is nothing hidden that will not be disclosed, and nothing concealed that will not be known or brought out into the open' (Luke 8:17). When he comes in judgement upon the Edomites he is going to go straight to their prized possessions and pillage them! (v. 6).

4. They will discover that their former friends will turn against them. They had made pacts with some of the surrounding nations. They had eaten bread with them (v. 7). These people had been their companions. However, like David,

they were soon going to discover that 'Even my close friend, whom I trusted, he who shared my bread, has lifted up his heel against me' (Psalm 41:9). These 'friends' are going to deceive them (v. 7). They will plot against Edom with such cunning that the Edomites will not know anything about it. These 'friends' will overpower them and force them to the border of their land. In fact during the first half of the fifth century raiders came in from the desert. These Nabateans threw out the Edomites, who were forced to move southwards. Later, in 125 BC, they (or the Idumeans as they were then called—King Herod was an Idumean) were overthrown and to all intents and purposes disappeared, just as God had said they would in verse 10, where we read, 'You will be destroyed for ever.' All that is now left on the site to remind us of them is the 'stark wilderness and the most isolated emptiness'. Stuart Briscoe tells us that 'Petra is one of the most formidable, forsaken spots on the earth.'

5. 'In that day'—the day of God's judgement, the Lord is going to 'destroy the wise men of Edom' and all the 'men of understanding in the mountains of Esau' (v. 8). The wise men on whom they relied would be powerless to help them. They would all be destroyed.

6. Even the brave warriors of the land 'will be terrified' (v. 9). Teman was one of the important cities of Edom, known for its wise men (see Jeremiah 49:7). In the book of Job we read that one of his 'comforters', Eliphaz, came from Teman (Job 2:11). But because the people of Edom trusted in their own strength, rather than in the Lord, they were utterly destroyed.

What can we learn from this?

1. Pride goes before a fall
If any of us are proud of our achievements, and seeking our own glory in them, then we are in trouble. Proverbs 3:5 says,

'Trust in the LORD with all your heart and lean not on your own understanding.' Those who think that they are so clever that they can manage without God are in for a terrible shock on the Day of Judgement.

2. God will be vindicated

We are foolish if we think that we can go through life ignoring God and his Word. The people of Edom were destroyed and humiliated because they refused to listen to God. All our sins will have to be paid for. If we think we can brave it out and persuade God not to punish us because we assume that we have been 'good', then we are in for a great shock.

When the Tent of Meeting was erected in the desert the Israelites were told that they must not go near it, 'or they will bear the consequences of their sin and will die' (Numbers 18:22). This is the message all the way through the Bible. Sin must be punished with death. It is no use saying, 'God is a God of love. He won't send anyone to hell.' If we even think such things we are rejecting the Word of the Lord.

God kept his word of judgement in regard to Edom, and he will do so in regard to every sinner. The only hope for any sinner is to flee to the rock which is higher than ourselves (Psalm 61:2). That rock is the Lord Jesus Christ. The only safety we can find from the storm of judgement is in him.

The Edomites believed that they would be as exalted as the eagle, but only those who hope in the Lord will renew their strength. Only they will soar on wings like eagles. Only they will run and not grow weary, and only they will walk and not be faint (see Isaiah 40:31).

24

Do not gloat over the misfortunes of your brothers

Please read Obadiah 10–14

I n the year 1887, in the Norwegian town of Fyresdal, a baby boy was born and named Vidkun. When he left school he joined the army and eventually rose to the rank of major. He was appointed as an official in the League of Nations and from 1927–1929 he had the special care of British interests in Russia. He entered parliament and became defence minister of Norway in 1931. Three years later he founded his own political party, which he called the National Socialists, in imitation of the German National Socialist party. Having a firm belief in fascism, he aided the Nazi invasion of Norway in 1940. He did this by delaying mobilization and urging non-resistance. As a reward for his help in conquering Norway, Hitler made him prime minister.

However, his actions angered most of his fellow Norwegians, and when the war ended in May 1945 Vidkun Quisling (for that was his full name) was arrested and tried. He was found guilty of treason and executed in that same month. Ever since then the name of 'quisling' has become a byword for a citizen who aids an occupying force to conquer his own country, and thus betrays his brothers. Edom was a brother-nation of Judah (which was all that was left of Israel by this time), and in this book of Obadiah we see how Edom acted as a 'quisling' centuries before Vidkun Quisling was born!

The reason why the Edomites were going to come under God's judgement was because they had failed to come to the aid of their brother-nation, Judah. They had not only neglected to help the people of Judah, but had actually betrayed them in their hour of great need. Calvin points out that these invaders were 'foreigners'. They were people who came from a great distance, but Edom was not only a nation who lived nearby in geographical terms; the people were of the same blood as Israel. This being the case, they ought to have come to the aid of Judah, but instead they stood and watched, and even gloated over the downfall of their brother-nation.

If we are correct in assuming that Obadiah's prophecy was written following Jerusalem's destruction by the Babylonians, it means that these events took place some two hundred years after the northern kingdom of Israel had been deported, never to return. By this time the southern kingdom, Judah, had been greatly depleted and its capital city of Jerusalem lay in ruins.

To the south of Judah lay the mountain kingdom of Edom, sometimes called Mount Seir. It is against these Edomites that Obadiah directs his prophecy, but he utters it in the hearing of the remaining people of Judah—the remnant of Israel. He does this as an encouragement to the Jews, so that they might know that the Lord had not deserted them, despite their sinful ways.

In the previous chapter we looked at the pride of Edom; in this one we shall see how they behaved towards their brother-nation, Judah, and what God said he would do about their treachery.

Edom's violence against his brother (v. 10)

It is often said that 'Blood is thicker than water.' This means that there is a special bond between family members. They may fall out among themselves, but what happens if someone from outside the family tries to malign a family member? In most cases the members of the family stick together. Even if they have not spoken to one another for years, they will almost always defend each other against an attack from outside. That is what we mean when we say, 'Blood is thicker than water.'

However, in Edom we have the case of a family member that failed to keep to this convention. Not only did Edom not spring to the defence of Judah when the latter was attacked, but he actually exacted violence against his 'brother Jacob'. Unfortunately this kind of behaviour was a family trait, and like all family feuds, this one had gone on for generations. It went right back to the time of the birth of the founders of their two nations, Esau and Jacob.

When these twin brothers were still in the womb of their mother, Rebekah, the Bible tells us that they jostled with each other. Rebekah was worried about this and asked God why it was happening to her. The Lord replied:

> Two nations are in your womb,
>   and two peoples from within you will be separated;
> one people will be stronger than the other,
>   and the older will serve the younger   (Genesis 25:23).

We can trace the years of hostility which had gone on right up to the time of Obadiah's prophecy by looking at the following scriptures: Genesis 27:41-45; 32:1-21; 33; 36; Exodus 15:15; Numbers 20:14-21; Deuteronomy 2:1-6; 23:7: 1 Samuel 22; Psalm 52; 2 Samuel 8:13-14; 2 Kings 8:20-22; 14:7; Psalm 83; Ezekiel 35; Joel 3:18-19; Amos 1:11-12; 9:12. Although Jacob was far from perfect, he had been called by God to be the father of the great nation of Israel. Long before that time God had told his grandfather Abraham, 'All peoples on earth will be blessed through you' (Genesis 12:3). But Esau had always shown hostility to God's choice of his brother rather than himself. Now, in the days of Obadiah, at long, long last, the descendants of this antagonistic brother, Edom, were about to reap the reward for all this history of shameful behaviour.

The people of Judah are told, through Obadiah, that Edom would be 'covered with shame' because of 'the violence' that they had inflicted against their 'brother Jacob'. In the Bible shame is usually associated with nakedness but here Edom is told that he will be covered—not with garments, but with shame!

This line of enmity had continued right down to the days of Obadiah. Although the nation of Edom has been lost without trace for very many centuries, we can still see this same kind of hostility between nations and individuals continuing right down to the present day. Jacob (or Judah), whose other name was Israel (which means a prince with God), represents God's people, and Edom stands for the world, and all those who follow the world's system of thinking and behaviour. The people of God, for all their faults, still belong to him and, in their better moments, they do seek to walk humbly with God and obey his Word. But the people of this world ignore God and his ways. Like Edom of old, they are proud and arrogant. They care nothing for God, his people or the things of God. The Bible is nothing but a dusty old book to them. With all their scientific achievements, they behave as though they were the kings of the universe. They think that they are soaring on high far above everyone else, and no one can bring them down to the ground. As with Edom of old, God declares to all unbelieving people today, 'You will be destroyed for ever.'

Edom's behaviour outlined (11-14)

God's judgement is always associated with 'the day'. In the five verses under consideration in this chapter, we have 'the day' mentioned eight times. Verse 11 tells of 'the day you stood aloof'. In verse 12 we read of 'the day of his misfortune', 'the day of their destruction' and 'the day of their trouble'. In verse 13 it is called 'the day of their disaster' three times and, finally, in verse 14 the prophet speaks of 'the day of their trouble'.

What was the reason for the judgement on Edom? Why was their nation going to be destroyed for ever? It was because of their violent behaviour towards God's people, especially in the incident referred to here, the destruction of Jerusalem.

Verses 11-14 tell us what the people of Edom did when Jerusalem was sacked. This is referred to in Psalm 137 and Ezekiel 35. Here, in verse 11 of Obadiah, we are told that they 'stood aloof while strangers carried off his wealth and foreigners entered his gates and cast lots for Jerusalem'. While foreigners were desecrating the holy city and destroying it, all that the people of Edom did was to 'stand aloof'.

They behaved as the priest and the Levite did in the parable of the Good Samaritan: they passed by on the other side (Luke 10:31-32). In fact, the Edomites behaved in an even worse way: they actually watched what was happening. They looked on with glee, while Israel was treated atrociously. In fact they 'were like one of them' (i.e. the invaders). Even though they did not appear to take an active part in the destruction of Jerusalem, they might just as well have done so, because they in effect took the side of the invaders. When strangers carried off the wealth of Israel the Edomites did nothing to stop them. Instead of sympathizing with their brothers, they gloated over their downfall. They actually rejoiced over the misfortune of the people of Judah. They looked down on their brothers. They were glad to demean them and boasted in the day of their trouble (v. 12).

They went even further: they marched through the gates of Jerusalem and looked down on their brothers in the day of their calamity. It seems that they may even have joined in the looting of the city, for we read that they seized the wealth of the people of Judah (v. 13).

We do not know whether they actually took part in the desecration of the temple (described in 2 Kings 25:13-17) and stole any of its treasures. If they did they were not only stealing from God, but were disobeying the Lord's command, because only priests were allowed to enter the Holy Place, and only the high priest could go into the Holy of Holies.

Yet even that was not the full extent of their treachery. Some of the citizens of Jerusalem managed to escape the swords of the Babylonians, but as they ran out of the cities they found the Edomites waiting at the various crossroads to intercept them. The Edomites would have been better placed than the Babylonians to know the routes which the fugitives were likely to take, and they either cut them down and killed them, or handed them over to the Babylonians (v. 14).

This means that although, strictly speaking, the Edomites themselves were not attacking Israel, they were aiding and abetting their conquerors. Therefore, they were cowards. 'To attack Israel was to attack God's purpose for the world.' Israel was God's chosen people. In Deuteronomy 32:10 we read:

In a desert land [God] found him,
    in a barren and howling waste.
He shielded him and cared for him;
    he guarded him as the apple of his eye.

In Psalm 17:8 we see David being pursued by his enemies, and he prays, 'Keep me as the apple of your eye; hide me in the shadow of your wings.'

In *The Hiding Place*, the film about the experiences of the Ten Boom family during Hitler's occupation of Holland, their pastor is asked to smuggle a Jewish baby into the countryside so that he can escape the clutches of the Nazis. But the pastor refuses, saying that it is against the new law, which the Germans had passed concerning the Jewish people. Papa Ten Boom replies, 'He that harms him touches the apple of God's eye.'

So, in turning against Israel Edom had gone against the Word of God and his purposes for the whole world. God was going to say to them, 'As you have done, it will be done to you; your deeds will return upon your own head' (v. 15).

Lessons for us in our day
Edom had totally violated the covenant of brotherhood. Even human covenants are important to God, and they should be to us as well. Edom was antagonistic towards his brother Israel. We should not behave in the same way. Even though great difficulties arise in our lives, we should stick to our word, regardless of the problems.

This applies to marriage vows. It holds for God's laws regarding the relationship between parents and children. Neighbours and their rights should be respected, and nations should support and encourage right relationships between them.

Edom forgot that God will have his day. They were only

interested in their day, but God will be vindicated. The nation, or the individual, that forgets God is in for a very great shock one day. The Day of the Lord is coming when we shall all be judged.

In verse 17 of Obadiah we see that it is only 'on Mount Zion' that there 'will be deliverance'. Mount Zion reminds us of Jerusalem, the holy city. It was outside the walls of that city that the Lord Jesus Christ was hung up on a cross to die. This was so that all those who have faith in him might be saved from all their sins, and might enjoy the blessings of life eternal.

25

The kingdom will be the Lord's

Please read Obadiah 15–21

In many businesses today we find that various people often vie for positions of leadership; such people go about building their own little 'empires', and woe betide anyone who tries to stand in their way! It happens in the public sector, too, as some people in senior positions behave all the time as though they are watching their backs, and become jealous of any employee who has greater expertise than themselves in a particular area.

The ambition to be at the top of the tree is something which has been around for centuries. The little country of Edom, some six hundred years before the birth of Christ, was very proud and had no desire to be subject to any other nation, but God had other views. Because of the Edomites' antipathy to their brother-nation, Israel, and because of their arrogant attitude of self-sufficiency, the Lord declared that they were going to be destroyed.

In this closing section of Obadiah's prophecy we learn how

God was going to bring this about. The last words of this little book are: 'And the kingdom will be the LORD's.' This is echoed in Psalm 24:1 where we read, 'The earth is the LORD's and everything in it, the world, and all who live in it.' This prophecy demonstrates to Edom, and to all the surrounding nations, that the Lord is going to have dominion over all things. If we turn to the last book in the Bible, we shall learn that one day the kingdoms of the world will become the kingdom of our Lord and of his Christ, 'and he will reign for ever and ever' (Revelation 11:15).

Wrongs will be put right (vv. 15–16)

Obadiah once again speaks of 'the day of the LORD.' In verse 8 he had spoken about the day when he would destroy all those in leadership in Edom. When we looked at that verse we saw that the Day of the Lord is a day of judgement. On that day he will demonstrate his power and his authority over all creation. That day will be a day to be feared. We are told that, as Edom had treated Israel, so the Lord will treat them in the same way: 'As you have done, it will be done to you; your deeds will return upon your own head' (v. 15).

In the prophecy of Ezekiel we read about this same punishment in relation to the people of Edom. The whole of Ezekiel chapter 35 is given over to a denunciation of Edom (also called Mount Seir), and we have something similar in Isaiah 34:8–15. In Ezekiel we read, 'Because you harboured an ancient hostility and delivered the Israelites over to the sword at the time of their calamity, the time their punishment reached its climax, therefore as surely as I live, declares the Sovereign LORD, I will give you over to bloodshed and it will pursue you. Since you did not hate bloodshed, bloodshed will pursue you' (Ezekiel 35:5–6).

As we come to verse 15 of Obadiah we see that something else is added to the picture. We discover that this Day of the Lord was not something far off that they did not need to think about for a long time. It was not like death—something that we do not dwell on because we hope that it lies far off in the future. This day, says Obadiah, 'is near'. Furthermore it will be 'for all nations'. In that day all of the enemies of God and his people will drink the cup of God's wrath. Often when we read about drinking in the Bible, it is related to judgement. Jeremiah tells us, 'This is what the LORD, the God of Israel, said to me: "Take from my hand this cup filled with the wine of my wrath and make all the nations to whom I send you drink it. When they drink it, they will stagger and go mad because of the sword I will send among them' (Jeremiah 25:15–16).

We have something similar in Jeremiah 49:12, which is also directed to Edom: 'This is what the LORD says: "If those who do not deserve to drink the cup must drink it, why should you go unpunished? You will not go unpunished, but must drink it."' Most familiar of all, we have the case of Jesus praying in the Garden of Gethsemane, when he was faced with having to pay the price of punishment for the sins of the world. He prayed, 'Father, if you are willing, take this cup from me; yet not my will, but yours be done' (Luke 22:42).

The Edomites had drunk 'on [God's] holy hill'. We do not know whether this was something that they did literally. They may have invaded the holy place and drunk from the wine that was there, but we have no evidence that they did so. However, they certainly watched with glee as the Babylonians ransacked Jerusalem. They had stood and watched and drunk in what they saw.

'Now', says the Lord, 'because of your sinfulness, you, and all other nations like you, are going to drink of my wrath. In fact, you are going to get so drunk that you will stagger around and be destroyed so thoroughly that it will appear as though you had never existed.'

That is the bad news in this section, but then we read some good news.

Deliverance will be found only on the hill of the Lord (vv. 17–18)

Jerusalem was built on two small hills. At one end was David's old capital city, Mount Zion. This lies outside the present wall of Jerusalem, which was built in the sixteenth century AD. At the other end stood Mount Moriah. That was the site where Solomon had built his temple. But the whole of Jerusalem was considered to be God's holy city. Verse 17 tells us three things about this city. First, Obadiah says that there 'will be deliverance' found in it. Secondly, we are told that 'It will be holy'; and thirdly, 'Jacob' (i.e. Israel) 'will possess' it as their 'inheritance', in accordance with God's promises of old.

Before this deliverance comes about we read of the terrible destruction which will come on the enemies of God's people. We read there about two houses carrying out this devastation. First there is 'the house of Jacob', and second, we have 'the house of Joseph'. We see that these two houses are going to be united in their attack upon Esau. Jacob's other name was Israel. We can see, then, that Obadiah is speaking here about the southern kingdom of Judah—that is, the remaining two tribes of Israel.

Joseph had two sons, Ephraim and Manasseh. Two different tribes grew from these ancestors. Both tribes represented their father, Joseph, who was so important in the book of Genesis. Therefore, when Obadiah speaks of 'the house of Joseph' he was referring to the northern kingdom of Israel. Long years before, these two parts of the country had become two separate areas, but now we learn that they will again be reunited in their attack upon Edom.

How were they going to wreak all this havoc? They were both very weak. The northern kingdom had been deported to Assyria, never to return, and the southern kingdom had been taken to Babylon as captives.

We can try to imagine how these words would have sounded in the ears of the exiled people of Judah, as they may have heard them in their captivity. They were demoralized and cut off from their beloved city of Jerusalem. They found it very difficult to praise God in their exile. Their lament occurs in Psalm 137: 'By the rivers of Babylon we sat and wept when we remembered Zion.' They cried out, 'How can we sing the songs of the LORD while in a foreign land?' (Psalm 137:1, 4). surely they must have been uplifted in their spirits as they heard about this scene depicting the whole of Israel, north and south, united together and going forward to burn up their enemies.

Many years before this, speaking through Moses, the Lord had said:

A fire has been kindled by my wrath,
　　one that burns to the realm of death below.
It will devour the earth and its harvests
　　and set on fire the foundations of the mountains
(Deuteronomy 32:22).

The Lord Jesus Christ uses this same figure when he speaks of the fires of hell, which are ever burning (e.g. Mark 9:48).

Edom, the old enemy of Israel, is depicted as stubble left in a field, after the wheat has been gathered. The reunited house of Israel will come and burn it up, utterly consuming it. God's people are going to set a fire alight which will consume all evil, so that no**n**e will survive. Such prophecies must have inspired God's feebl**e** p**eo**ple. God was not only going to bring them back to their be**l**ove**d** land; he was going to use them to bring about his purpos**e**s a**n**d set up his kingdom so that all the earth will be the kingdo**m** of the Lord.

We find this fulfilled in some measure in New Testament times. Jesus ca**m**e to 'bring fire on the earth' (Luke 12:49). He was going to br**i**ng victory over Satan, sin and this world, by dying on the cross to take away the sins of his people and rising again for their ju**s**tification. Afterwards two of his disciples said, 'Were not our h**ea**rts burning within us while he talked with us on the road a**n**d opened the Scriptures to us?' (Luke 24:32). In our days, 'Christ's Spirit purifies, refines, radiates from us, and brings warmth to others through us.'

Like the p**eo**ple of Obadiah's day, we live in a world which abounds in wickedness. So how are we going to be filled with such a spirit, which desires to carry out God's will? Like the people of Obadiah's day, we shall find such freedom only as we come to Mount Zion. 'On Mount Zion will be deliverance' (v. 17). Those who flee to this holy mountain will be saved. What, then, does this Mount Zion represent? It is the city of Jerusalem.

Even in our days, some 2,500 years later than this prophecy, Jerusalem is a divided city. It is a special holy place for three different religions—Christian, Jewish and Islamic. Temple Mount is the third most holy place for Muslims, and no Orthodox Jew will go up on to it for fear of treading on the place where the Holy of Holies once stood. And, in any case, it is under the jurisdiction of Muslims; it is the site of the Al Aqsa mosque and the magnificent Dome of the Rock.

So what does Obadiah's prophecy mean for us? In Galatians 4:25–26 we read about the contrast between the earthly

Jerusalem and the heavenly Jerusalem. Paul tells us that 'The Jerusalem that is above is free.' This means that, for us, coming to Mount Zion is coming to Christ. God's people of old had this promise that they would return to Jerusalem and possess its inheritance, but there was a condition attached to it. The prophet declares that this Mount Zion 'will be holy'. Therefore, the citizens of this Mount Zion will be those who have been cleansed from their sins. Their one desire will be to be wholly dedicated to the Lord and his service.

The whole land will be under God's rule (vv. 19–21)

By the time the Babylonians attacked Jerusalem the remnant of the Israelites had been scattered. Some went to the south (the Negev). Certain ones went to the various foothills of the mountains. Some hid in various places in Canaan, and others fled far to the north to Sepharad; some scholars believe this was Sardis in Asia Minor—that is, in modern Turkey.

When God comes to bring deliverance, all of these scattered peoples will return to their homeland. Those who have been sheltering in the desert of the Negev will take up residence in the mountains of Edom; they will become the rulers of that now deserted place. Others, who had been in hiding in the foothills, will go to different parts of the promised land. Some will go to Philistia (to the south-west of Israel) and others 'will occupy the fields of Ephraim and Samaria'. This means that they will settle in the land which had been occupied by the northern kingdom before they were transported to Assyria. Those exiles from Jerusalem who had been in far-off Turkey will go down to take over the Negev. In other words, God will bring about a great transformation in bringing in his kingdom of righteousness.

Finally, 'Deliverers' (the same word as was used for the judges of old) 'will go up on Mount Zion.' Their task will be 'to govern the mountains of Esau'—that means to rule over all those who had formerly been worldly in their attitude and deeds. This wonderful transformation will come about because 'The kingdom will be the LORD's.' The scene which Isaac Watts describes will then come to fruition:

> Jesus shall reign where'er the sun
> Doth his successive journeys run:
> His kingdom stretch from shore to shore,
> Till moons shall wax and wane no more
>
> (Isaac Watts, 1674–1748).

What does all this mean to us? It means that we should not try to be masters of our own destiny. Rather we should humbly seek to be under the rule of Christ. He said, 'seek first his kingdom and his righteousness, and all these things [that you have been worrying about] will be given to you as well. Therefore do not worry about tomorrow' (Matthew 6:33–34).

In the last book of the Bible we read that 'There were loud voices in heaven, which said: "The kingdom of the world has become the kingdom of our Lord and of his Christ, and he will reign for ever and ever" ' (Revelation 11:15). The Lord Jesus Christ wants to reign in our lives, but the load of sin that we carry has come between our God and us. However, out of his great heart of love, the Lord God Almighty has sent a deliverer. Just outside the walls of Jerusalem he was hung up on a cross and he died to pay the price for sin. The statement, 'On Mount Zion there is deliverance,' applies to the salvation which Christ's atoning death purchased for his people.

Although Edom was wicked and was destroyed, Amos 9:12 suggests that there was a small remnant of the people who did survive. How could that have been? It can only mean that they came to Mount Zion and found salvation there—even for

Edomites, who repented of their sin. In Joel 2:32 we read these words:

> Everyone who calls
> on the name of the LORD will be saved;
> for on Mount Zion and in Jerusalem
> there will be deliverance,
> as the LORD has said,
> among the survivors
> whom the LORD calls.